Contents

1. Origins 9
2. Standard Discussion . . . 23
3. Grooming the
   Samoyed 31
4. Your New Samoyed
   Puppy 37
5. Obedience Training . . . 54
6. Breeding Your Dog . . . 64
7. Care of the Mother and
   the New Family 79
8. General Health Care . . 87
9. Dog Show
   Competition 103
10. Building a Kennel and
    Exercise Runs 111
11. Mental and Physical
    Good Health 121

Suggested further reading to follow up Mrs. Reynaud's book: *The Complete Samoyed*—Bob and Dolly Ward; *The Dog In Action*—McDowell Lyon; *Dog Steps*—Rachel Page Elliot; *The New Knowledge of Dog Behavior*—Clarence Pfaffenberger; *Training You To Train Your Dog*—Blanch Saunders; and *Practical Dog Breeding and Genetics*—Elanor Frankling.

Photo credits: All color photographs and pages 18 (top), 30, 45, 46, 47, and 116 by Vince Serbin; pages 8 and 22 by William Gilbert; pages 5, 33, and 42 by T. Schupan-Image II; page 41 by John Ashbey; page 117 by Mary Ann Catalde; page 125 by Brian Haffey; page 44 by Louise Van der Meid. Mr. Serbin's photos were made possible through the courtesy and cooperation of Joyce Reynaud, Silversea Samoyeds, Howell, New Jersey; Patricia Kirms, Wall, New Jersey; James and Beverly Novonglosky, Bordentown, New Jersey.

ISBN 0-87666-680-2

Distributed in the UNITED STATES by T.F.H. Publications, Inc., 211 West Sylvania Avenue, Neptune City, NJ 07753; in CANADA by H & L Pet Supplies Inc., 27 Kingston Crescent, Kitchener, Ontario N2B 2T6; Rolf C. Hagen Ltd., 3225 Sartelon Street, Montreal 382 Quebec; in ENGLAND by T.F.H. Publications Limited, 4 Kier Park, Ascot, Berkshire SL5 7DS; in AUSTRALIA AND THE SOUTH PACIFIC by T.F.H. (Australia) Pty. Ltd., Box 149, Brookvale 2100 N.S.W., Australia; in NEW ZEALAND by Ross Haines & Son, Ltd., 18 Monmouth Street, Grey Lynn, Auckland 2 New Zealand; in SINGAPORE AND MALAYSIA by MPH Distributors Pte., 71-77 Stamford Road, Singapore 0617; in the PHILIPPINES by Bio-Research, 5 Lippay Street, San Lorenzo Village, Makati, Rizal; in SOUTH AFRICA by Multipet Pty. Ltd., 30 Turners Avenue, Durban 4001. Published by T.F.H. Publications Inc., Ltd., the British Crown Colony of Hong Kong. THIS IS THE 1983 EDITION.

SAMOYEDS

by Joyce Reynaud

◄ 1

2

In (1) and (2) modern day
Sammys display the
"smile" that is the
hallmark of their breed.
Though rarely used today
for work as rugged as their
sled-pulling ancestors who
enabled some of the first
explorers to the North and
South poles to chart those
areas, present day Sammys
are still known for their
willingness to work.
(3) This Samoyed
youngster chews on a
Nylabone, a ham-flavored
nylon product safe for
dogs because it will not
chip or splinter.

3

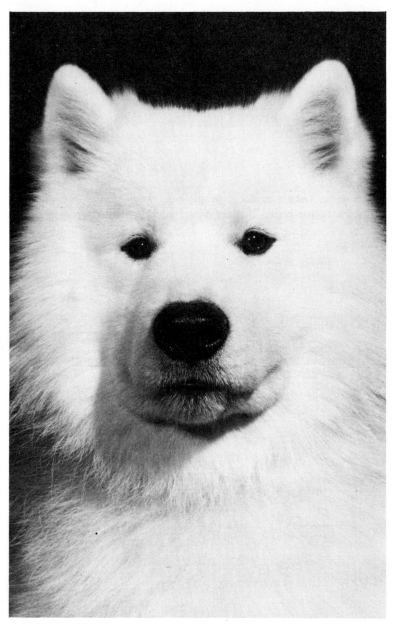

Ch. Silver Sea Summer Thunder, a representative of the breed, preserving some of the best characteristics of the early Bjelkier dogs who accompanied the Samoyede Eskimos in their nomadic travels across the Arctic wastes.

1. ORIGINS

In the vast frozen wasteland of the Arctic, there dwelt a good-natured people called Nentzi—also known as *Samoyede*—(pronounced SAM A YED') and their wonderful *Bjelkier*, white dogs that bred true.

HISTORY

Samoyedes were a nomadic people who were hunters and reindeer herdsmen. Their prized Bjelkier dogs could be counted upon to fall in equally well as either hunter or herdsman, and in addition fill in as a sled dog when the occasion demanded.

It's interesting to note that within the territory of Northern Russia, from the White Sea, east across the Ural Mountains, to the Yenise River, there could be found brown and white, black and white and even all black dogs that looked like the all-white Bjelkier, but were Ostiak and Laika dogs out of the Archangel territory

The Samoyedes were unique among Eskimo people in that they had a close personal relationship with their dogs, as well as a working one. It was known that, often, family members would each take a dog into the large tents they lived in (called Chooms), which were made of reindeer skin, and let the dog sleep with them under their reindeer skin robes for extra warmth. Children were allowed to play with the pups and women often raised the litters, even nursing a pup if the dam, for one reason or another, was unable or unavailable to do so herself. This fact points up how much the Samoyede people prized these dogs and socialized them.

In spite of their gentleness with their dogs and their good-natured ways, the Samoyedes were a very primitive people and it was not unusual to see the white fur pelt of an incapable worker adorning a woman's coat (called Panza) or serving as chaps-like leggings on the men. Some early visitors to the Arctic tell of the dogs having been shorn like sheep.

It isn't clear whether the Samoyede people had a breeding program but we do know that the beautiful fluffy white Samoyed (the final 'e' was dropped in England by the Kennel Club in 1923, and by the American Kennel Club in 1947) dates as far back as one thousand years before Christ, setting it among the world's oldest known breeds. We also know that the natives often refused to sell their dogs when explorers and traders began to move into the territory, and dogs were often "spirited" away via dubious routes.

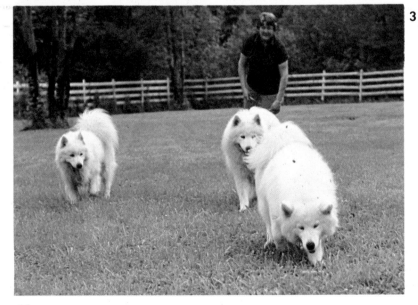

(1) The Samoyed pup, though frolicsome and curious as the healthy pup of any breed, still has an essentially quiet, calm temperament much in evidence. This pup is content to lie in his mistress' lap, rather than struggling to be down and off. (2) Translated from the frozen, snowy habitat of their origins, the Samoyed is able to adapt well, keeping a few considerations in mind. Bred for hard work and endurance, the Sammy has moderate exercise needs that must be met to keep the dog in tone and good spirits. The large grassy enclosed area pictured is an ideal arrangement for the breed, allowing maximum opportunity for exercise without the necessity of taking him for a walk several times a day. This owner has started a game of chase to initiate the exercise session. (4) While their heavy coats provide natural insulation against heat, they also automatically supply warmth both summer and winter. After rigorous exercise, supply the dogs with an ample source of cold fresh water.

4

ANCIENT LEGENDS

Even before the time the Samoyedes migrated from the territory where their ancestors travelled, there is evidence that these people—then located in Central Asia—shared their lives with their dogs. Legend tells of a desert people who, some 35,000 years ago, were driven by enemies northward through Mongolia and finally to the frozen fortress of the Arctic.

The story also tells of a biscuit-colored dog, whose fur was bleached by the Arctic sun after he left the desert, and was tipped with the silvery glisten of the frozen land he finally came to occupy.

Through this constant close relationship with man over the centuries, there evolved a rugged breed that would work toe-to-toe with man, lend comfort in the home, fight fiercely in battle and work side-by-side with the master it was his desire to please. The Samoyed will never take orders subserviently. He is a great fun-loving animal, retaining much of the happy-go-lucky nature of his primitive progenitors.

THE EXPLORERS

It's no wonder that the European explorers of the late 19th century, whose lives were intertwined with these dogs, became deeply touched by them. And indeed, it was one of these explorers, Dr. Fridtjof Nansen, the Norwegian explorer, who was most responsible for introducing to the world the Bjelkier—the white dog with the smiling face.

Nansen set sail to find the North Pole on a ship of his design, called the *Fram*, in 1893. In his written account of the perilous journey, he makes many references to his dogs. These were procured for him by his broker, Alexander Trontheim. Trontheim was a native of Tobolsk, Siberia, and knew of the Samoyedes and their dogs.

Nansen was so pleased with the sled dogs Trontheim brought to him that Nansen recommended Trontheim to many other explorers of the time. Trontheim supplied many of these explorers with Samoyeds for their sledding expeditions in the regions of the polar caps, both North and South.

Though most of Nansen's dogs were lost during the years of searching for the elusive North Pole, a few of the dogs left on the *Fram* were brought back to Norway. There is no record of these dogs and it is not known whether or not they ever sired any offspring. There seems to be no indication that they did.

While Nansen was responsible for introducing the Samoyed to the Western World, it was Frederick Jackson who explored Franz Joseph Land, a group of islands belonging to the U.S.S.R. in the Arctic Ocean, with dogs procured by Trontheim, who brought his expedition dogs home to England.

And so it was that Jackson presented a dog named Jaco to Queen Alexandra and gave several others to Mr. and Mrs. E. Kilburn-Scott, in 1899. After his return to England, he became the first president of the Samoyed Association, a position he was to hold for eighteen years.

There are so many wonderful stories told by the explorers at the turn of the century, that anyone truly seeking the depth of affection the magnificent white dogs could command from even these most rugged of individuals, will find further reading a must.

The history of the breed would lack the final luster without mention of the Norwegian explorer Roald Amundsen. Amundsen was the first to reach the South Pole on December 14, 1911.

Significant to the history of the Samoyed breed was the fact that Amundsen's lead dog on the expedition was a Samoyed female, named Etah. Indeed, it was Etah who was the first of a team of Samoyeds to set paw across the South Pole.

The Antarctic explorer, Sir Ernest Shackleton, in his observations of sled dogs, notes the intelligence of the Samoyeds used on his expedition of 1901-1903. He tells of the Samoyed ingenuity at ducking out to their kennels and looking totally innocent after having committed a forbidden act.

And there is the tale of Antarctic Buck, one of the dogs that returned with the Borchgrevink Antarctic expedition in 1900. He was placed in the Sydney, Australia, zoo as an exhibit. Mrs. Clara Kilburn-Scott took pity on the dog and prevailed upon her husband to use his influence to rescue the dog. After several attempts, the Kilburn-Scotts were able to bring Buck back to England. There he sired two litters before a fatal bout with distemper took his life. Even so, Buck distinguished himself as a force in the breed and many of today's champions can trace their lineage back to him.

ROOTS IN ENGLAND

The breed was put into good hands with the Kilburn-Scotts. Their kennel prefixes—Polar, Farningham and Arctic—can be traced to the foundations of the champions of today. The line travels through one great champion, sire and dam, after another.

There are some records of black, deep biscuit and black with white colored dogs owned by the Kilburn-Scotts, but these were not the Bjelkier from the White Sea and were soon eliminated from the breeding stock.

Mrs. Kilburn-Scott has been heralded for her never-ending attention to the excellence that established the firm roots and foundation stock upon which this beautiful breed has been built.

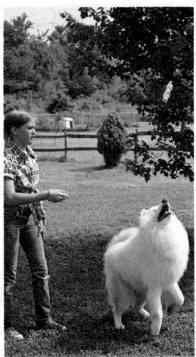

1
2

(1) The Samoyed is not only a willing worker, but also an eager play-mate. (2) The Samoyed was one of few northern breeds that enjoyed a close personal relationship with their Eskimo companions. These nomadic people revered their dogs as workers and companions. The loyal, loving ways that won the Sammy a respected position among the Samoyede people make him a highly desirable companion in to-day's homes. This Sam participates in a game of catch with his young mistress. (3) Puppies usually do not need baths, and the coat of the Samoyed has natural resistance to soiling; even so a white-coated puppy seems to invite double jeopardy. If your pup tries to dig his way out of an outdoor kennel and becomes a walking mudpie in the endeavor, then a bath is in order. (4) It is important that your Samoyed, puppy or adult, is completely dried after a bath. Most of the excess water can be toweled off and the job finished up with a hair dryer. (5) A young Sam with an admirer. The young man is strong enough to support this half-grown dog's weight; very small children should not pick the dog up once he has reached this size.

14

3

4

5

OFF TO AMERICA

This precocious pup of the Arctic not only won over the tough early explorers, and thus a new home in England, but also won over a beautiful princess and yet another home, this time in America.

Mercy d'Argenteau was the Princess de Montyglyon. The Princess was known to exhibit Collies and Chows all over Europe. While exhibiting in Russia in 1902, Princess de Montyglyon found a handsome Samoyed following her down one of the aisles, dragging his benching chain behind. Upon returning the dog, the Princess found he was Russian Champion Moustan, one of the Samoyeds owned and exhibited by the Grand Duke Nicholas, the Czar's brother. The next day Ch. Moustan once again broke loose from his bench to follow the Princess.

The Grand Duke was also charmed by the lovely Princess de Montyglyon and upon her departure by rail from St. Petersburg, she found at her disposal one of the imperial coaches. Inside the coach there was a large basket of flowers and Champion Moustan—a gift from the Duke.

Two years later Mercy d'Argenteau brought Moustan and three other Samoyeds to America. A son of Moustan, Champion de Witte of Argenteau, became the first Samoyed Champion of Record in 1907.

It was the Princess also to whom Roald Amundsen, the Norwegian explorer, presented Etah, his Samoyed lead from his famous South Pole expedition.

THE FIRST BEST IN SHOW

It took a little better than forty years from the first Samoyed Champion to the first Best in Show Sammy. And what a win it was! A female from the classes by the name of Sweet Missy of Sammar won the title on April 10, 1949.

There have been more than two dozen Samoyeds to earn the coveted Best in Show since 1949, but only one kennel, the Wychwood Kennel owned by the late Mrs. Bernice Ashdown, has earned the honor of Best in Show with four different Samoyeds. The BIS winners were: Ch. Princess Silvertips of Kobe (bitch), Ch. Silver Spray of Wychwood (dog), Ch. Silver Scion of Wychwood (dog) and Ch. Americ of Kobe (dog).

Together with trainer-handler, Charles Rollins, Mrs. Ashdown elevated the Samoyed to a serious contender in the breed ring and in the obedience ring as well. Wychwood earned the first Companion Dog Excellent and Utility Dog Tracker titles. Champion Rimsky of Norka was the first dog to win a CDX while Champion Marina of Wychwood became the first female in the breed to earn a Companion Dog title (Marina's grandsire, Champion Anastasia's Rukavitza, C.D., was the first Samoyed to earn the title).

STILL IN HARNESS

With most of our present-day dogs descended from expedition dogs, it's no wonder that they feel at home in a harness. However, the Samoyed temperament calls for special training techniques and no one is more capable of explaining these basics to the neophyte than sledding expert Mrs. Judy Schirber.

The author is truly indebted to Mrs. Schirber for taking the time to share her experience, so that the reader can know and enjoy his or her Samoyed that much more.

THE SAMOYED AS A RACING DOG

by Mrs. Judy Schirber

Ed. note: Mrs. Schirber and her husband have been handling Samoyed racing teams for approximately ten years. At the time of this writing, theirs was one of only a few teams of Samoyeds in racing competition.

There have been various arguments over the years as to whether or not the Samoyed can be used as a sprint racer. To my way of thinking, all those qualities that made the Samoyed a useful herd dog originally can be put to use training the dog to become a sprint racer. The herd dog had to be intelligent enough to understand some form of command, had to be light on his feet and agile enough to withstand sharp, right-angle turns. And the dog had to be fast enough to outrun and head off reindeer.

Training the Samoyed to run is done differently than training any other northern breed of dog. The Samoyed runs to please his master; the Siberian Husky runs for the sheer love of running. A good age to begin training your Samoyed is when he is still a puppy. He has to always believe it is fun to run, or he will lose interest. Shortly after the puppy is leash trained and knows enough to respond to his name, after he has become settled in his new home and is well used to everyone, is the time to begin his training as a sprint racer. (The same applies if you are only interested in recreation running and not competitive racing). So sometime between the age of eight and twelve weeks a small harness of canvas webbing should be placed on the puppy for short intervals, to get him used to wearing it. He should not be allowed to wear it without supervision and never should he be allowed to chew on it. (Harnesses of canvas webbing are used, never leather, for pulling purposes).

When the puppy is used to wearing the harness without biting or scratching at it, the next step is finding a very lightweight object to tie to the ring normally at the back of the harness, just before the tail. We've used

1

2

(1) Samoyed puppies at this age—six to eight weeks— are malleable little creatures, capable of a high degree of geniality and learning. The skills learned are dependent upon the natural tendencies bred into their lines and the teaching capabilities of the handler. Sammys learn readily if the learning is fun. When it becomes burdensome, they lose interest. (2) The Samoyed accustomed to a constant cold climate will develop a shaggy heavy coat to satisfy his needs for warmth and protection. If your Samoyed is to be an outdoor dog, he should not be haphazardly transferred from outdoor living to indoor living and back. (3) In this Samoyed belonging to Mrs. Jean Blank, the full-coated beauty of the breed is readily apparent.

a lightweight block of wood or even an empty airline bag. Your puppy should be wearing a leather collar along with his harness (NOT a choke collar). Clip his leash to his collar and say, "O.K. (dog's name), let's go!" and run alongside him, holding his leash. Have him pull the object you've attached to his harness, which is just light enough so he can feel a little pull behind him. If he will not run with you at first, have someone he knows squat down several feet ahead of him and call him. When he begins to pull and run willingly, praise him by saying, "Good boy" and use his name. When you want him to stop, say, "Whoa" and his name and at the same time, you stop running. Never step on the object he is pulling and make it so heavy that he can't pull it easily. He must always think running and pulling is fun. This is the Samoyed mentality. He will never do anything willingly that doesn't appeal to him and isn't fun.

When he is running with you willingly, you can unleash him and allow him to run in a confined area on his own, pulling the object. The sessions should be short to retain his enthusiasm. When he is pulling, you should drop back so you are behind him and give him the commands from there.

When your puppy is older, you can make the object he is pulling a little heavier. Make sure the harness always fits and does not rub or chafe, especially between the forelegs. We always keep harnesses in various sizes to fit our dogs as they grow. A small puppy-size harness can be made from a webbing material. When your dog is mature, usually a male at a year and a half and a bitch at 11 months, you can order a custom-made harness to fit your dog's measurements.

A word about your dog's weight here. Keep your puppy's (and your adult Samoyed's) weight down. A fat adult dog attempting to run, may wind up with a heart attack. A slim dog lives longer, is healthier, and can run faster. A normal racing weight for a medium-boned, twenty-inch adult bitch (twenty inches from the withers or shoulder blades to the ground), is thirty-five to forty pounds. A good weight for a twenty-two inch adult male is forty-five to fifty pounds.

By the time your dog is five months old, he or she is capable of pulling a normal car tire with ease, providing the dog has had previous training. Remember too, that the pulling is done with the chest muscles, not with the rear legs. If the pulling is properly supervised, it will not hurt the puppy. All the training sessions should be brief for the puppy and young dog and all of them should end while the dog is still happy and enthusiastic. Serious training can begin around seven months and should be done on a one-to-one basis with you on foot behind your dog.

In training the older dog, care should be taken to keep the dog's weight down and articles being pulled should not bounce into his feet or legs when running. Weight should always be added gradually, over a period of months and training should always be in cool weather. It can be accomplished in the summer if it is done in the morning or early evening.

In areas where there is no snow or before the snow falls, three-wheeled rigs are used to train sled dogs. Lightweight rigs can be made from used bicycle parts. They should always have a brake, a steering device and a bumper guard of some sort. They usually look like a type of tricycle and have a platform on which the driver stands. The same applies to a sled. It must have a brake, but your bodyweight and balance act as the steering mechanism in this case. A dog sled also has a bumper. Neither the rig nor the sled should be allowed to run into the dog. This will discourage him from pulling. Never run more dogs than you can control by yourself. Sled dogs should be taught from the very first that the only order of business in harness is running and not playing. Your dogs should always realize that the lead-dog is YOU and that you do not tolerate anything less than seriousness in harness.

If you are training more than one dog to run at once, each dog should receive individual training, then they should be placed together to run. We usually don't have our young dogs running in front of a wheeled rig before seven months and then we hook up two youngsters with an experienced adult leading. Our seven-month-olds are not run more than one-quarter of a mile to begin with. A young dog of a year and a half is capable of racing with two others in the three-dog class for three miles, with the proper training.

Samoyeds have been used for ski-joring, freight hauling, weight pulling, long-distance racing as well as sprint racing.

There are many organizations and publications devoted to sled dog racing. A few that the Samoyed owner interested in training his dog for actual runs may find helpful are:

The International Sled-Dog Racing Association seeks to standardize race rules through the racing world. Membership entitles one to its newsletter, "INFO." (Ivan and Kathy Beliveau, R.F.D. 4, Box 305B, Manchester, N.H. 03102.)

The Organization for the Working Samoyed is devoted to all working aspects of the breed. A newsletter is published every three months. (Bruce Berryman, treasurer, The Fieldstones, Stoddartsville, Star Route 1, P.O. Box 39, Blakeslee, Penna. 18610.)

Team and Trail is a monthly magazine which publishes a full worldwide schedule of sled-dog races every fall, in addition to ads for harnesses and other equipment (c/o Cindy Molburg, Center Harbor, N.H. 03226.)

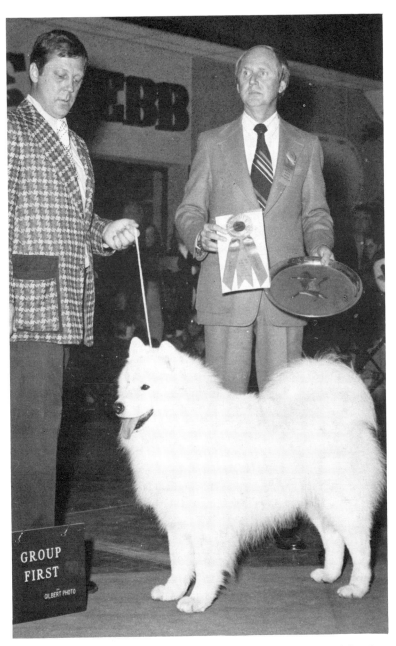

Ch. Silversea's Ivan of Arandale, owned by Lois Kraemer of Bordentown, New Jersey, is shown taking a Group First at a recent kennel club show.

2. STANDARD DISCUSSION

So there's a standard. So what. You're not into breeding and the breed has gotten along for thousands of years without it. Don't forget though, that even the early Samoyed had a criteria of some sort, and those specimens that didn't measure up wound up adorning m'ladies wardrobe.

A NEW NAME AND A STANDARD

The Bjelkier was re-named Samoyede, after the people from whom it came, by the English zoologist, Ernest Kilburn-Scott. The Kilburn-Scotts became the founders of the breed as we know it today. It was the explorer Frederick Jackson who obtained a great many Samoyeds for Kilburn-Scott during the early part of the twentieth century.

The first written standard was painstakingly set down by Ernest Kilburn-Scott to introduce you to your Samoyed, and to preserve those qualities that make the breed so special. By knowing the standard for the breed you have a working measure of the quality of the pup you choose, and the dog you own.

STANDARD IN AMERICA

The American Kennel Club standard for the Samoyed is one of the most explicit for the breed anywhere in the world and is generally hailed as being among the best written.

Samoyeds were introduced to America in 1906 by the Princess de Montyglyon, but it was 1923 before the Samoyed Club of America was formed and the first official standard adopted. Up until that time the English standard was used. The American standard is presented later in this chapter and may be used as a general reference for the British version as well, since there are but few major variations.

OTHER LANDS

Australia still uses the English standard. The basics are the same, except that the standard size for dogs and bitches is an inch shorter than the American standard calls for. The English standard, rather than disqualifications, has a list of faults.

Canada has kept the English size requirements, but expanded the sections on general conformation, gait and head detail. The Canadian standard includes a list of disqualifications, as does the American standard, but with the addition of rear dew claws as a further disqualifying fault.

REVISIONS
Things were moving along for the Samoyed in the United States. The breed had moved from the Miscellaneous Class to the Non-Sporting Group among breeds officially recognized by the American Kennel Club. But the Westminster Show of 1923 became a fiasco, when the judge withheld the Reserve Winners Dog and Reserve Winners Bitch because he asserted they were not true Samoyeds. The dogs in question had been recently imported from the Kilburn-Scott kennel.

It was at that point that breed enthusiasts banded together to form the Samoyed Club of America and adopted the English standard as the criteria by which the Samoyed would be bred as well as judged. By the end of World War II breed enthusiasts were once again discontent with the way the breed was being judged at all-breed shows, so they set out to clarify the standard. After twelve years and the taking of measurements and angles of literally hundreds of dogs, a new standard was adopted. That was in 1957; the last revision in 1963 was only to drop a point scale which was thought to be misleading.

GENERAL APPEARANCE
The wonderful personality of the Samoyed has evolved from untold centuries of close contact with man. An irritable or shy Samoyed should *never* be used to perpetuate the breed.

Grace, dignity, and strength, all wrapped up in a glistening spikey white outer coat and a softer under coat define the general appearance of the Samoyed. The male will shed, usually, once a year and the female twice. That double coat acts as a good insulator, retaining warmth in winter and keeping heat out in summer. The Northern breeds have the best "air conditioning" system of all breeds. They can withstand the drastic sub-zero temperatures of the Arctic winters as well as the heat of the Tropics.

CONFORMATION
As a herding dog, the Samoyed is a dog of moderate size and moderate bone. Those who have massive bone are those who break down under heavy working conditions. Those of fine boning, can't keep pace. Leg hair, as a dog matures, is what gives the illusion of heavy bone.

HEAD
How wise the early standard planners were in setting down one head

description to call for proportion rather than specific measurements. This allows latitude for the variation found, without giving up the all-important Samoyed expression. This expression is most delightfully described in the history of the breed as found in the official standard for that breed. The final lines in the accompanying general description read, "the big white dog carries in its face and heart the spirit of Christmas the whole year through." Looking at a Samoyed should make you want to smile because he is smiling at you.

Samoyeds have erect ears that are well covered with hair. This is to keep the ears from freezing in the Arctic. While pups at three months or so seem to grow "jack-rabbit" ears, they usually are in proportion by adulthood.

Those nice, dark brown, deep-set, almond eyes help prevent snow blindness and protect against the Arctic winds.

TORSO

The proud, erect neck of the Samoyed is not only a breathtaking thing of beauty to behold, but also the framework for the *cervical ligament,* a part of which supports the front muscles of the shoulder. These front muscles provide the pull-power when the Samoyed is hauling a sled.

The Samoyed, when viewed from the side looks almost square. That is, his body looks roughly as long as he stands high at the shoulder. He has a strong, well-sprung, deep chest with ample heart and lung room. Females are a little longer to accommodate the bearing of puppies. A dog with a long back is weak and rendered unable to work efficiently. A shallow or narrow chested dog without good heart and lung room would tire easily. The chest should not be a barrel chest. This would cause the dog to throw his elbows out as the shoulder blade moved back and forth. This causes a serious loss of efficiency in movement.

MOVEMENT

The Samoyed should be an agile dog of smooth movement—not bouncy like a hackney pony. This ease of motion, combined with a well layed-back shoulder and well bent stifle, allows this working dog to cover the most amount of ground in the fewest possible steps. This, in turn, allows for great endurance.

The dog with, say, only a 52° shoulder layback and an equal bend of stifle behind, is to be favored over the dog with a 45° layback in front but only 52° in rear. This is because the *balanced* dog can work more efficiently than the one that must first take care of the business of compensating for his own lack of balance before he can get on with his work.

TAIL

A dog uses his tail for balance while running. The Northern dog, when lying down or sleeping, wraps his tail around his face to insulate against Arctic sub-zero temperatures. So his tail should be of good length and well-plumed. One Arctic explorer made the mistake of docking his dogs' tails—and the dogs soon died of pneumonia!

In total, the Samoyed, for all his look of elegance and luxury, can get out there and work with the best of them—and the best for him is to be able to work with and please you.

AMERICAN STANDARD FOR THE SAMOYED

General Conformation:

(a) General Appearance: The Samoyed, being essentially a working dog, should present a picture of beauty, alertness and strength, with agility, dignity and grace. As his work lies in cold climates, his coat should be heavy and weather-resistant, well groomed, and of good quality rather than quantity. The male carries more of a "ruff" than the female. He should not be long in the back as a weak back would make him practically useless for his legitimate work, but at the same time, a close coupled body would also place him at a great disadvantage as a draft dog. Breeders should aim for the happy medium, a body not long but muscular, allowing liberty, with a deep chest and well-sprung ribs, strong neck, straight front and especially strong loins. Males should be masculine in appearance and deportment without unwarranted aggressiveness; bitches feminine without weakness of structure or apparent softness of temperament. Bitches may be slightly longer in back than males. They should both give the appearance of being capable of great endurance but be free from coarseness. Because of the depth of chest required, the legs should be moderately long. A very short-legged dog is to be deprecated. Hindquarters should be particularly well developed, stifles well bent and any suggestion of unsound stifles or cowhocks severely penalized. General appearance should include movement and general conformation, indicating balance and good substance.

(b) Substance: Substance is that sufficiency of bone and muscle which rounds out a balance with the frame. The bone is heavier than would be expected in a dog of this size but not so massive as to prevent the speed and agility most desirable in a Samoyed. In all builds, bone should be in proportion to body size. The Samoyed should never be so heavy as to appear clumsy nor so light as to appear racy. The weight should be in proportion to the height.

(c) Height: Males—21 to 23½ inches; females—19 to 21 inches at the withers. An oversized or undersized Samoyed is to be penalized according to the extent of the deviation.

(d) **Coat (Texture & Condition):** The Samoyed is a double-coated dog. The body should be well covered with an undercoat of soft, short, thick, close wool with longer and harsh hair growing through it to form the outer coat, which stands straight out from the body and should be free from curl. The coat should form a ruff around the neck and shoulders, framing the head (more on males than on females). Quality of coat should be weather resistant and considered more than quantity. A droopy coat is undesirable. The coat should glisten with a silver sheen. The female does not usually carry as long a coat as most males and it is softer in texture.

(e) **Color:** Samoyeds should be pure white, white and biscuit, cream, or all biscuit. Any other colors disqualify.

Movement:

(a) **Gait:** The Samoyed should trot, not pace. He should move with a quick stride that is well timed. The gait should be free, balanced and vigorous, with good reach in the forequarters and good driving power in the hindquarters. When trotting, there should be a strong rear action drive. Moving at a slow walk or trot, they will not single-track, but as speed increases the legs gradually angle inward until the pads are finally falling on a line directly under the longitudinal center of the body. As the pad marks converge the forelegs and hind legs are carried straight forward in traveling, the stifles not turned in nor out. The back should remain strong, firm and level. A choppy or stilted gait should be penalized.

(b) **Rear End:** Upper thighs should be well developed. Stifles well bent—approximately 45 degrees to the ground. Hocks should be well developed, sharply defined and set at approximately 30 per cent of hip height. The hind legs should be parallel when viewed from the rear in a natural stance, strong, well developed, turning neither in nor out. Straight stifles are objectionable. Double-jointedness or cowhocks are a fault. Cowhocks should only be determined if the dog has had an opportunity to move properly.

(c) **Front End:** Legs should be parallel and straight to the pasterns. The pasterns should be strong, sturdy and straight, but flexible with some spring for proper let-down of feet. Because of depth of chest, legs should be moderately long. Length of dog from the ground to the elbow should be approximately 55 per cent of the total height at the withers—a very short-legged dog is to be deprecated. Shoulders should be long and sloping, with a layback of 45 degrees and be firmly set. Out at the shoulders or out at the elbows should be penalized. The withers separation should be approximately 1-1½ inches.

(d) Feet: Large, long, flattish—a hare-foot, slightly spread but not splayed; toes arched; pads thick and tough, with protective growth of hair between the toes. Feet should turn neither in nor out in a natural stance but may turn in slightly in the act of pulling. Turning out, pigeon-toed, round or cat-footed or splayed are faults. Feathers on feet are not too essential but are more profuse on females than on males.

Head:

(a) Conformation: Skull is wedge-shaped, broad, slightly crowned, not round or apple-headed, and should form an equilateral triangle on lines between the inner base of the ears and the center point of the stop. *Muzzle:* Muzzle of medium length and medium width, neither coarse nor snipy; should taper toward the nose and be in proportion to the size of the dog and the width of skull. The muzzle must have depth. *Stop:* Not too abrupt, nevertheless well defined. *Lips:* Should be black for preference and slightly curved up at the corners of the mouth, giving the "Samoyed smile." Lip lines should not have the appearance of being coarse nor should the flews drop predominately at corners of the mouth.

Ears: Strong and thick, erect, triangular and slightly rounded at the tips; should not be large or pointed, nor should they be small and "bear-eared." Ears should conform to head size and the size of the dog; they should be set well apart but be within the border of the outer edge of the head; they should be mobile and well covered inside with hair; hair full and stand-off before the ears. Length of ear should be the same measurement as the distance from inner base of ear to outer corner of eye.

Eyes: Should be dark for preference; should be placed well apart and deep-set; almond shaped with lower lid slanting toward an imaginary point approximating the base of ears. Dark eye rims for preference. Round or protruding eyes penalized. Blue eyes disqualifying.

Nose: Black for preference but brown, liver, or Dudley nose not penalized. Color of nose sometimes changes with age and weather.

Jaws and Teeth: Strong, well-set teeth, snugly overlapping with scissors bite. Undershot or overshot should be penalized.

(b) Expression: The expression, referred to as "Samoyed expression," is very important and is indicated by sparkle of the eyes, animation and lighting up of the face when alert or intent on anything. Expression is made up of a combination of eyes, ears and mouth. The ears should be erect when alert; the mouth should be slightly curved up at the corners to form the "Samoyed smile."

Torso:

(a) Neck: Strong, well muscled, carried proudly erect, set on sloping shoulders to carry head with dignity when at attention. Neck should blend into shoulders with a graceful arch.

(b) Chest: Should be deep, with ribs well sprung out from the spine and flattened at the sides to allow proper movement of the shoulders and freedom for the front legs. Should not be barrel-chested. Perfect depth of chest approximates the point of elbows, and the deepest part of the chest should be back of the forelegs—near the ninth rib. Heart and lung room are secured more by body depth than width.

(c) Loin and Back: The withers forms the highest part of the back. Loins strong and slightly arched. The back should be straight to the loin, medium in length, very muscular and neither long nor short-coupled. The dog should be "just off square"—the length being approximately 5 per cent more than the height. Females allowed to be slightly longer than males. The belly should be well shaped and tightly muscled and, with the rear of the thorax, should swing up in a pleasing curve (tuck-up). Croup must be full, slightly sloping, and must continue imperceptibly to the tail root.

Tail: The tail should be moderately long with the tail bone terminating approximately at the hock when down. It should be profusely covered with long hair and carried forward over the back or side when alert, but sometimes dropped when at rest. It should not be high or low set and should be mobile and loose—not tight over the back. A double hook is a fault. A judge should see the tail over the back once when judging.

Disposition: Intelligent, gentle, loyal, adaptable, alert, full of action, eager to serve, friendly but conservative, not distrustful or shy, not overly aggressive. Unprovoked aggressiveness to be severely penalized.

DISQUALIFICATIONS
Any color other than pure white, cream, biscuit, or white and biscuit. Blue eyes.

A FINAL WORD ABOUT STANDARDS

If you plan to enter your Samoyed into show competition or you wish to consider serious breeding of your Samoyed, you should become thoroughly familiar with the official standard of the national club under which your dog is registered.

Even if you do not desire to show or breed your Samoyed (and instead want simply a beloved household pet or a working dog), you likely would be interested in knowing about those attributes that exemplify the perfect dog.

For the sake of brevity, only the American Kennel Club standard was presented in this book. For the standard approved by any other national club, write to the appropriate office.

The author, pictured with one of her fine Samoyeds. To keep the Samoyed's coat its whitest between infrequent baths, brush in cornstarch and talcum powder, making sure to brush the mixture out thoroughly afterwards.

3. GROOMING THE SAMOYED

A glistening white coat, almost pristine in its after-bath cleanness, is one of the hallmarks of a Samoyed. Surely a well-groomed Samoyed is the most breath-taking sight in all dogdom. The admiration your meticulously groomed Sammy will draw, even from the most non-doggy folks, is worth what small portion of your day it will take to keep him looking his best.

Because a "Sammy" has no doggy odor and because his coat will shed most dirt, daily brushing with a pin brush is usually all it takes to maintain an immaculate dog.

EQUIPMENT

The bare-bones essentials are a good pin brush, slicker brush, and good nail clipper. Nice to have, are a stainless steel comb with coarse and fine teeth, a natural bristle brush, scissor and thinning sheers. Absolute luxury means a grooming table, professional blow dryer on a stand and a nail grinder.

GETTING STARTED

Most Samoyed puppies have had some grooming, as the little rascals were probably digging up the breeder's favorite garden display before you came to see them and have had at least one bath already.

Grooming, however, does not begin with a bath, but rather with daily brushing. You will find that your pup will learn to love it, too. Adult Samoyeds have been known to jump up on their grooming table—or any table available—in eager expectation of their grooming routine.

A stand-off coat is brushed in the direction of tail to head. Just the opposite direction of the way the hair lies. The actual method is to take the pin brush in one hand and with the other hand hold the coat down. Starting at the neck, just behind the ears, part a section from ear to ear and with a lifting motion, from the skin out, brush forward. When you're satisfied there's no loose hair or matted fur left, make a second part about an inch further down the neck. Continue brushing up and out from the skin to the tip of the fur, right on down to the base of the tail. The dog can sit or stand. When you brush the dog's sides and around the under part of the neck and chest, it's convenient to have the dog lie on his side, although it's not essential.

The Samoyed tail is a beautiful plume. When brushing it take care not to rip the fur. The dog's tail is a more sensitive area and gentle brushing is required here. Starting at the base and brushing from the skin out, use the same parting method all the way around until you get to the tip.

On the legs, lift the feathering up and brush from the bottom of the leg to the elbow in front and from the hock to the rump in the rear, still taking one small section at a time to insure that all loose hair and mats are removed.

Now you're ready to clip the toe nails. Grasp the foot firmly but gently in one hand and with the other clip the clear tip off where the nail hooks slightly. You can see the quick in a Samoyed's nail. Take care not to cut it or the toe will bleed quite profusely. Such bleeding can easily be stopped by using a styptic pencil at the point of bleeding.

TRICKS AND TIPS

There's an axiom around the grooming tents at the dog shows that says, "Never brush a dry coat." You are less likely to rip the fur and the end result gives a nice stand-off effect if the coat is slightly moistened before brushing. This grooming trick can be accomplished with a plastic trigger-spray bottle of cold water—the colder the better. Set the spray on "fine mist." A light misting of the area you are working on will make the end product a beautifully polished, stand-off coat.

Quick cleaning between baths can be accomplished by sprinkling the coat with a 50-50 mixture of corn starch and talcum powder. Just be sure to brush all the powder out, as a powdered coat is not allowed in the show ring. Another excellent, quickie-cleaning solution is Kote-Glo. This is a liquid cleaner/conditioner that is quick drying and need not be rinsed out. Take a towel and soak it with the cleaner, rubbing briskly back and forth over the entire coat. Then rub again with a dry towel and brush dry.

A Sammy who is shedding can develop mats, especially behind the ears, along the neck, back, tail, leg feathering and underside of the belly. This is where deft hand work is useful. Most mats can be worked out with your fingers by gently pulling them apart, and the loose hair removed.

Tougher knots will require a de-tangler. You can make your own by mixing one part Wella Balsam with three parts water and using your trigger spray. You can also buy a professional de-tangler from your pet supplier. First spray the matted area and work as before.

A really tough mat that won't respond to treatment will usually give way to the "divide and conquer" method. This takes skill and care not to cut the dog. Slip one blade of a partially opened pair of scissors under the mat near the skin. Cutting through the mat with the scissors in a vertical

The truly well-groomed Samoyed can be kept so by a daily, brief brushing with a pin brush. Mats, which can be a problem in long-coated breeds, will not be if he is brushed regularly.

position, simply divide the mat into smaller sections. Then resume working the smaller mats apart with your fingers. Be absolutely certain that no skin is between the scissor blades before you cut! Remember, if you brush your dog frequently, you won't have this problem.

There are times when a once-glistening white coat just won't come up white. This is the time to have your dog checked for worms or other health problems. If everything checks out try putting the dog on one teaspoon of corn oil daily and add a teaspoon of wheat germ to his diet. If the coat feels too dry, add a tablespoon of Wella Balsam to the spray mist you use during brushing. If the problem seems to be a stained coat, use a shampoo with a bluing agent. If the stain doesn't respond then make a paste out of beauty salon peroxide and Ivory Flakes. Spread the paste over the problem area and let it dry. Then rinse thoroughly and bathe the dog.

THE BATH

Once all the loose hair is brushed out, you are ready to bathe your Samoyed. Place a skid-proof mat in the tub, so he won't slip. Have a good dog shampoo on hand, or a mild liquid, non-detergent soap, a short bristled brush to scrub extra dirty hocks, a spray attachment for the faucet, mineral oil—a few drops in the eyes—two large wads of cotton for the ears and lots of towels!

Begin wetting the coat with tepid, not hot or even warm water. Start behind the ears and work down the neck and back. Apply shampoo liberally over the wet area. Scrub, getting your fingers down to the skin. Wet and scrub again, working loose any stubborn dirt. Work under the neck and chest, down the shoulders and sides, the front legs, elbows, under the belly and back legs and feathering. Wet the tail and shampoo the top and bottom sides of it.

Now you are ready to wash the ears and face. It is not desirable to put shampoo inside your dog's ears. This is where the wads of cotton come in. Put a cotton wad in each ear to prevent the shampoo from going in while you are bathing the dog. Shampoo the stand-up portion of the ear and later wipe the inside of the ear—only the part you can see—with a soft moist cloth. You will find that a no-tears baby shampoo on the face is a good idea until your dog and you have more of an idea of how the bath proceeds.

Notice that there was no instruction to fill the tub. It's better to let the water run slowly from the spray and leave the drain open. Many puppies are terrified and never learn to enjoy their bath because they slipped and immersed their heads in the water.

RINSING

Begin by getting a good grip on the fur under the chin and carefully rinse the face with slow-running water. Start with the cheeks and top of the head, ears and muzzle. Talk to your puppy and reassure him all the time and at the same time, hold him firmly so the pup doesn't make for the hills, leaving you to ponder the error of your ways, while he splatters shampoo all over the house. If water gets in the puppy's eye, wipe it out with your finger, across the closed eyelid, as you would your own eye.

Once the face is done, turn the water pressure up for a good strong spray that will get through that dense coat. Adjust the temperature to make sure that the water is still tepid. Rinse from the back of the ears down the neck in the same pattern used to shampoo. Rinse, rinse, rinse! Make sure that all the shampoo is removed so as not to cause a skin irritation. Don't forget the bottom of the feet, around the testicles of the male and vulva of the female. Shoulders and bellies seem to hide the most shampoo, so check carefully in these areas.

Once you're satisfied that all the shampoo is out, run water over the dog and squeeze the fur to see if any hidden soap surfaces. If it doesn't, take the cotton out of the ears, squeeze off the excess water from the legs and towel dry. Let the dog shake and then towel again. Shaking brings the water to the ends of the hair and helps to dry the dog. A gentler toweling is in order for puppies, but older dogs usually enjoy a brisk rubdown.

Drying can be accomplished after towel drying by simply brushing and air drying if the weather is mild. Or if the weather is too cool for that, you can set the dog on a grooming table and use a hand dryer or a professional model dog dryer on a stand, if you have one.

When introducing a puppy to a blow dryer it's a good idea to hold him on your lap and blow dry everything but his face. Remember to blow the coat in the same direction in which you've learned to brush it.

TRIMMING

Whiskers on the Samoyed are always left on when the dog is being shown in England or Canada. It is strictly a matter of preference. Most Samoyeds (that are shown) in the United States are trimmed. Use a good hair-cutting shear and trim the whiskers close to the face. There are usually two or three long eyebrow hairs. These are trimmed, too. Any very long, wispy hairs sticking out of the ears can be trimmed into line with the overall shape. The feet are trimmed close around the nails and excess fur on the bottom of the foot is cut close to the pads. The hair on the hocks is combed to stand out and then cut straight and close with thinning scissors to give a clean, tidy look to the rear legs.

The end result will give you a great feeling of pride and joy when you see the most beautiful of all canines standing before you. Remember, too, that Samoyeds have been sharing with their owners for time untold, so be sure to share that pride with him. Tell him how handsome he looks. Samoyeds like compliments, too!

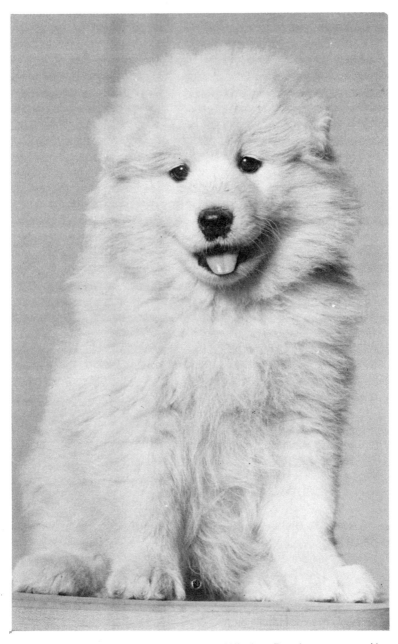

This captivating youngster, Holihouse Witches Prophasey, owned by Patricia A. Eik, Trenton, New Jersey, now possesses his conformation championship and CD title.

4. YOUR NEW SAMOYED PUPPY

PREPARING FOR THE SAMOYED PUPPY'S ARRIVAL

In choosing a puppy, be certain beforehand that each member of the family is truly enthusiastic about having this particular breed of dog as an addition to their circle. Dogs are much too intelligent not to sense whether or not they are liked. If your puppy feels unwanted, you may find an unhappy dog on your hands that could easily turn into a "problem child." Before buying, research the breed and make sure it is the one for you. Besides reading, a good way to learn about your prospective pet is to observe one of the same breed in its permanent home surroundings. Most owners will be only too happy to show off their furry friend.

One of the most important factors to consider when selecting a dog, whether it is to be a pet or show dog, is its temperament. When looking at a litter of puppies for a prospective purchase, spend time just quietly observing them. Usually the most outgoing or aggressive puppy is your best bet. However, do not overlook the more reserved puppy. Most dogs are wary of strangers, so reserve may indicate caution, not timidity. He may calmly accept your presence when he senses that all is well. In any event, never force yourself on a puppy—let him come to you. Beware of the puppy that hides in the corner and won't emerge until you have left. Chances are he will always be high-strung and may develop more undesirable habits as a result of his nervousness.

Because at least three out of four prospective purchasers of dogs want to buy a young rather than an adult or almost adult dog, the problem of preparing for the arrival of a permanent canine house guest almost always means preparing for the arrival of a puppy. This is not to say that there is anything wrong with purchasing an adult dog; on the contrary, such a purchase has definite advantages in that it often allows freedom from housebreaking chores and rigorous feeding schedules, and these are a definite benefit to prospective purchasers who have little time to spare. Since the great majority of dog buyers, however, prefer to watch their pet grow from sprawlingly playful puppyhood to dignified maturity, buying a dog, practically speaking, means buying a puppy. Before you get a puppy be sure that you are willing to take the responsibility of training him and caring for his physical needs. His early training is most important, as an adult dog that is a well-behaved member of the family is the end product of your early training. Remember that your new puppy knows only a life of romping with his littermates and the security of being with his mother, and that coming into your home is a new and sometimes frightening experience for him. He will adjust quickly if you are patient with him and show him what you expect of him. If there are small children in the family be sure that they do not abuse him or play roughly with him. A puppy plays hard, but he also requires frequent periods of rest. Before he comes, decide where he is to sleep and where he is to eat. If your puppy does not have a collar, find out the size he requires and buy an inexpensive one, as he will soon outgrow it. Have the proper grooming equipment on hand. Consult the person from whom you bought the puppy as to the proper food for your puppy, and learn the feeding time and amount that he eats a day. Buy him some toys—usually the breeder will give you some particular toy or toys which he has cherished as a puppy to add to his new ones and to make him less homesick. Get everything you need from your pet shop before you bring the puppy home.

MALE OR FEMALE?

Before buying your puppy you should have made a decision as to whether you want a male or female. Unless you want to breed your pet and raise a litter of puppies, your preference as to the sex of your puppy is strictly a personal choice. On the whole both sexes are pretty much the same in disposition and character, and both make equally good pets.

SHOW DOG OR PET?

It is well to define in your own mind the purpose for which you want a dog, and to convey this to the breeder. A great deal of disappointment and dissatisfaction can be avoided by a meeting of the minds between seller and buyer.

Although every well-bred healthy member of the breed makes an ideal companion and pet, actual pet stock is usually the least expensive of the purebred registered stock. The person who asks for a pet, pays a pet-geared price for the animal. Pet stock is least expensive because these dogs are deemed unsuitable for breeding or exhibition in comparison to the standard of perfection for the breed. Generally only skilled breeders and judges can point out the structural differences between a pet and show quality dog.

If you are planning to show your dog, make this clear to the breeder and he will aid you in selecting the best possible specimen of the breed. A show quality dog may be more expensive than one meant for a pet, but it will be able to stand up to show ring competition.

This lovely litter, whelped by Ch. Miss "Hollie" CDX, Can. CD, the dam owned by Patricia Eik of Trenton, New Jersey, can be typical of the quality of dogs a prospective owner will see if he has been careful to seek out conscientious breeders when he intends to buy a puppy.

WHERE TO BUY YOUR SAMOYED PUPPY

Once you have decided on the particular breed that you want for your pet, your task is to find that one special dog from among several outlets. Buying a well-bred, healthy dog is your foremost concern. By doing a little research in the various dog magazines and newspapers you can locate the names and addresses of breeders and kennels in your area that are known for breeding quality animals. The American Kennel Club will also furnish you with addresses of people to contact that are knowledgeable about your chosen breed.

Your local pet shop, although necessarily restricted from carrying all breeds in stock, may sometimes be able to supply quality puppies on demand. Due to the exorbitant amount of space and time needed to properly rear puppies, pet shops generally prefer to assist owners by supplying all the tools and equipment needed in the raising and training of the puppies. The pet shop proprietor, if unable to obtain a dog for you, can often refer you to a reputable kennel with which he has done business before.

SIGNS OF GOOD HEALTH

Picking out a healthy, attractive little fellow to join the family circle is a different matter from picking a show dog: it is also a great deal less complicated. Often the puppy will pick you. If he does, and it is mutual admiration at first sight, he is the best puppy for you. Trust your eyes and hands to tell if the puppy is sound in body and temperament. Ears and eyes should not have suspicious discharges. Legs should have strong bones; bodies should have solid muscles. Coats should be clean. Lift the hair to see that the skin is free of scales and parasites.

Reliable breeders and pet shops will urge you to take your puppy to the veterinarian of your choice to have the puppy's health checked, and will allow you at least two days to have it done. It should be clearly understood whether rejection by a veterinarian for health reasons means that you have the choice of another puppy from that litter or that you get your money back. Be sure to get the details of this policy before you purchase any puppy.

PAPERS FOR YOUR SAMOYED

When you buy a purebred dog you should receive his registration certificate (or an application form to fill out), a pedigree, and a health certificate made out by the breeder's veterinarian. The registration certificate is the official kennel club paper. If the puppy was named and registered by his breeder, you will want to complete the transfer and send it, with the stated fee, to the appropriate national club under which the

Ch. Silversea Winkbal Jesse Jane, going Best of Winners at a Potomac Valley Samoyed Club Specialty show. Jess won over 150 other dogs as well as bitches. She is an excellent example of the breed's outstanding style.

dog has been registered. They will transfer the dog to your ownership in their records and send you a new certificate. If you receive, instead, an application for registration, you should fill it out choosing a name for your dog, and mail it, with the fee, to the club.

The pedigree is a chart showing your puppy's ancestry and is not a part of his official papers. The health certificate will tell what shots have been given and when the next ones are due. Your veterinarian will be appreciative of this information, and will continue with the same series of shots if not completed.

REGISTERING YOUR PUPPY

For information on how to register a new litter of pedigreed dogs, owners may write to the following:

This pup, the Pines I'sis, belonging to Lois Kraemer, seems to have found a niche he is happy with. Unlike your new puppy he may never have had to leave his original home, and so he has never had to go through the adjustment of settling into a new family and surroundings. Be patient with your pup; don't add to his distress by scolding him for whining or expressing his loneliness for littermates the first night in a new home.

Though this litter may be registered with the AKC when you decide which puppy is for you, you will want to register it again under its own individual name showing yourself as owner.

American Kennel Club
51 Madison Avenue
New York, New York 10010
United States of America

Canadian Kennel Club
2150 Bloor Street West
Toronto, Ontario M6S 4V7
Canada

Australian Kennel Club
Royal Show Grounds
Ascot Vale, Victoria
Australia

British Kennel Club
1 Clarges Street
London, W1Y 8AB
England

THE PUPPY'S FIRST NIGHT WITH YOU

The puppy's first night at home is likely to be disturbing to the family. Keep in mind that suddenly being away from his mother, brothers, and sisters is a new experience for him; he may be confused and frightened. If you have a special room in which you have his bed, be sure that there is nothing there with which he can harm himself. If you want him to sleep in your room he probably will be quiet all night, reassured by your presence. If left in a room by himself he is likely to cry and howl, and you will have to steel yourself to be impervious to his whining. After a few nights alone he should adjust. The first night that he is alone it is wise to put a loud-ticking alarm clock, as well as his toys, in the room with him. The alarm clock will make a comforting noise, and he will not feel that he is alone.

YOUR PUPPY'S BED

Every dog likes to have a place that is his alone. He holds nothing more sacred than his own bed whether it be a rug, dog crate, or dog bed. If you get your puppy a bed be sure to get one which discourages chewing. Also be sure that the bed is large enough to be comfortable for him when he is full grown. Locate it away from drafts and radiators. A word might be said here in defense of the crate, which many pet owners think is cruel and confining. Given a choice, a young dog instinctively selects a secure place in which to lounge, rest or sleep. The walls and ceiling of a crate, even a wire one, answer that need. Once he regards his crate as a safe and reassuring place to stay, you will be able to leave him alone in the house.

FEEDING YOUR SAMOYED PUPPY

At the time of purchase, most breeders will give you food for a few days, along with instructions for feeding so that your puppy will have the same diet he is accustomed to until you can buy a supply at your pet shop.

Your pup will make the adjustment to new home and family more readily if he knows there is one place entirely his own, and that can always be found in the same spot where he expects to find it whatever the time or occasion.

44

If you own more than one dog, individual feeding bowls are a good idea once the dogs pass the young puppy stage. It is important that each gets a proper portion at feeding time; this may not be the case where a community feeding dish is used.

As a general rule, a puppy from weaning time (six weeks) to three months of age should be fed four meals a day; from three months to six months, three meals; from six months to one year, two meals. After a year, a dog does well on one meal daily. There are as many feeding schedules as there are breeders, and puppies do fine on all of them, so it is best for the new owner to follow the one given him by the breeder of his puppy. Remember that all dogs are individuals. The amount that will keep your dog in good health is right for him, not the "rule book" amount. A feeding schedule to give you some idea of what the average puppy will eat is as follows:

Morning meal: Puppy meal with milk.

Afternoon meal: Meat mixed with puppy meal, plus a vitamin-mineral supplement.

Evening meal: Same as afternoon meal, but without a vitamin-mineral supplement.

(1) The more people the pup is exposed to during his first months, the more companionable and well-adjusted will he be. This is especially important if he is to live in a house where there are children. (2) The ways in which he can be socialized will change as he grows. The type of game-playing this young girl and her dog engage in will reinforce the bond that began forming when he was much younger. (3) Don't expect overmuch from your puppy, or put him into a situation that will prove too great a temptation to his puppy instincts. If you don't want him to dig up your prize petunias, don't let him near them unattended. (4) Using bait, pieces of liver or other favorite treats, as a way to hold your dog's attention is one way to establish a learning pattern.

TRANSITIONAL DIET

Changing over to an adult program of feeding is not difficult. Very often the puppy will change himself: that is, he will refuse to eat some of his meals. He'll adjust to his one meal (or two meals) a day without any trouble at all.

BREAKING TO COLLAR AND LEASH

Puppies are usually broken to a collar before you bring them home, but even if yours has never worn one it is a simple matter to get him used to it. Put a loose collar on him for a few hours. At first he may scratch at it and try to get it off, but gradually he will take it as a matter of course. To break him to a lead, attach his leash to his collar and let him drag it around. When he becomes used to it pick it up and gently pull him in the direction you want him to go. He will think it is a game, and with a bit of patience on your part he will allow himself to be led.

DISCIPLINING YOUR SAMOYED PUPPY

The way to have a well-mannered adult dog is to give him firm basic training while he is a puppy. When you say "No" you must mean "No." Your dog will respect you only if you are firm. A six-to eight-week-old puppy is old enough to understand what "No" means. The first time you see your puppy doing something he shouldn't be doing, chewing something he shouldn't chew or wandering in a forbidden area, it's time to teach him. Say "No" firmly. Usually a firm "No" in a disapproving tone of voice is enough to correct your dog, but occasionally you get a puppy that requires a firmer hand, especially as he grows older. In this case hold your puppy firmly and slap him gently across the hindquarters. If this seems cruel, you should realize that no dog resents being disciplined if he is caught in the act of doing something wrong, and your puppy will be intelligent enough to know what the slap was for.

After you have slapped him and you can see that he has learned his lesson, call him to you and talk to him in a pleasant tone of voice—praise him for coming to you. This sounds contradictory, but it works with a puppy. He immediately forgives you, practically tells you that it was his fault and that he deserved his punishment, and promises that it will not happen again. This form of discipline works best and may be used for all misbehaviors.

Never punish your puppy by chasing him around, making occasional swipes with a rolled-up newspaper: punish him only when you have a firm hold on him. Above all, never punish you dog after having called him to you. He must learn to associate coming to you with something pleasant.

HOUSEBREAKING

While housebreaking your puppy, do not let him have the run of the house. If you do you will find that he will pick out his own bathroom, which may be in your bedroom or in the middle of the living room rug. Keep him confined to a small area where you can watch him, and you will be able to train him much more easily and speedily. A puppy does not want to dirty his bed, but he does need to be taught where he should go. Spread papers over his living quarters, then watch him carefully. When you notice him starting to whimper, sniff the floor or run agitatedly in little circles, rush him to the place that you want to serve as his relief area and gently hold him there until he relieves himself. Then praise him lavishly. When you remove the soiled papers, leave a small damp piece so that the puppy's sense of smell will lead him back there next time. If he makes a mistake, wash the area at once with warm water, followed by a rinse with water and vinegar or sudsy ammonia. This will kill the odor and prevent discoloration. It shouldn't take more than a few days for him to get the idea of using newspapers. When he becomes fairly consistent, reduce the area of paper to a few sheets in a corner. As soon as you think he has the idea fixed in his mind, you can let him roam around the house a bit, but keep an eye on him. It might be best to keep him on a leash the first few days so that you can rush him back to his paper at any signs of an approaching accident.

The normal healthy puppy will want to relieve himself when he wakes up in the morning, after each feeding and after strenuous exercise. During early puppyhood any excitement, such as the return home of a member of the family or the approach of a visitor, may result in floor-wetting, but that phase should pass in a few weeks. Keep in mind that you can't expect too much from your puppy until he is about five months old. Before that, his muscles and digestive system just aren't under his control.

OUTDOOR HOUSEBREAKING

You can begin outdoor training on a leash even while you are paper-training your puppy. First thing in the morning take him outdoors (to the curb, if you are in the city) and walk him back and forth in a small area until he relieves himself. He will probably make a puddle and then walk around, uncertain of what is expected of him. You can try standing him over a newspaper, which may give him the idea. Praise your dog every time taking him outside brings results, and he will get the idea. You'll find, when you begin the outdoor training, that the male puppy usually requires a longer walk than the female. Both male and female puppies will squat. It isn't until he is older that the male dog will begin to lift his leg. If you hate to give up your sleep, you can train your puppy to go out-doors during the day and use the paper at night.

ALL DOGS NEED TO CHEW

Puppies and young dogs need something with resistance to chew on while their teeth and jaws are developing—for cutting the puppy teeth, to induce growth of the permanent teeth under the puppy teeth, to assist in getting rid of the puppy teeth at the proper time, to help the permanent teeth through the gums, to assure normal jaw development and tó settle the permanent teeth solidly in the jaws.

The adult dog's desire to chew stems from the instinct for tooth clean-ing, gum massage and jaw exercise—plus the need for an outlet for periodic doggie tensions.

Dental caries as it affects the teeth of humans is virtually unknown in dogs—but tartar accumulates on the teeth of dogs, particularly at the gum line, more rapidly than on the teeth of humans. These accumulations, if not removed, bring irritation, and then infection which erodes the tooth enamel and ultimately destroys the teeth at the roots. Most chewing by adult dogs is an effort to do something about this problem for themselves.

Tooth and jaw development will normally continue until the dog is more than a year old—but sometimes much longer, depending upon the breed, chewing exercise, the rate at which calcium can be utilized and many other factors, known and unknown, which affect the development of individual dogs. Diseases, like distemper for example, may sometimes arrest development of the teeth and jaws, which may resume months, or even years later.

This is why dogs, especially puppies and young dogs, will often destroy property worth hundreds of dollars, when their chewing instinct is not diverted from their owner's possessions, particularly during the widely varying critical period for young dogs.

Saving your possessions from destruction, assuring proper develop-ment of teeth and jaws, providing for 'interim' tooth cleaning and gum massage, and channeling doggie tensions into a non-destructive outlet are, therefore, all dependent upon the dog having something suitable for chewing readily available when his instinct tells him to chew. If your pur-poses, and those of your dog, are to be accomplished, what you provide for chewing must be desirable from the doggie viewpoint, have the necessary functional qualities, and above all, be safe for your dog.

It is very important that dogs not be permitted to chew on anything they can break, or indigestible things from which they can bite sizeable chunks. Sharp pieces, from such as a bone which can be broken by a dog, may pierce the intestine wall and kill. Indigestible things which can be

Nylabone®, a unique 100 percent nylon chew bone, is the perfect chewing pacifier for young dogs in their teething stage, or even for older dogs to help satisfy that occasional urge to chew. Unlike many other dog bones on the market today, Nylabone® does not splinter or fall apart. It will last indefinitely and as it is used it frills, becoming a doggie toothbrush that cleans teeth and massages gums.

bitten off in chunks, such as toys made of rubber compound or cheap plastic, may cause an intestinal stoppage, if not regurgitated—to bring painful death, unless surgery is promptly performed.

Strong natural bones, such as 4 to 8 inch lengths of round shin bone from mature beef—either the kind you can get from your butcher or one of the variety available commercially in pet stores—may serve your dog's teething needs, if his mouth is large enough to handle them effectively.

You may be tempted to give your puppy a smaller bone and he may not be able to break it when you do—but puppies grow rapidly and the power of their jaws constantly increases until maturity. This means that a growing dog may break one of the smaller bones at any time, swallow the pieces and die painfully before you realize what is wrong.

Many people make the mistake of thinking of their dog's teeth in terms of the teeth of the wild carnivores or those of the dog in antiquity. The teeth of the wild carnivorous animals, and the teeth found in the fossils of the dog-like creatures of antiquity, have far thicker and stronger enamel than those of our contemporary dogs.

All hard natural bones are highly abrasive. If your dog is an avid chewer, natural bones may wear away his teeth prematurely; hence, they then should be taken away from your dog when the teething purposes have been served. The badly worn, and usually painful, teeth of many mature dogs can be traced to excessive chewing on natural bones.

Contrary to popular belief, knuckle bones which can be chewed up and swallowed by the dog provide little, if any, useable calcium or other nutriment. They do, however, disturb the digestion of most dogs and cause them to vomit the nourishing food they need.

An old leather shoe is another popular answer to the chewing need—but be very sure that the rubber heel, all nails, and other metal parts such as lace grommets, metal arches, etc., have been removed. Be especially careful to get all of the nails. A chunk of rubber heel can cause an intestinal stoppage. If it has a nail in it, the intestine wall may be pierced or torn. Then there is, of course, always the hazard that your dog may fail to differentiate between his shoe and yours, and eat up a good pair while you're not looking.

Dried rawhide products of various types, shapes, sizes and prices are available on the market and have become quite popular. However, they don't serve the primary chewing functions very well; they are a bit messy when wet from mouthing, and most dogs chew them up rather rapidly—but they have been considered safe for dogs until recently. Now, more and more incidents of death, and near death, by strangulation have been reported to be the result of partially swallowed chunks of rawhide swelling in the throat. More recently, some veterinarians have been attributing cases of acute constipation to large pieces of incompletely digested rawhide in the intestine.

The nylon bones, especially those with natural meat and bone fractions added, are probably the most complete, safe and economical answer to the chewing need. Dogs cannot break them or bite off sizeable chunks; hence, they are completely safe—and being longer lasting than other things offered for the purpose, they are economical.

Hard chewing raises little bristle-like projections on the surface of the nylon bones—to provide effective interim tooth cleaning and vigorous gum massage, much in the same way your tooth brush does it for you. The little projections are raked off and swallowed in the form of thin shavings—but the chemistry of the nylon is such that they break down in the stomach fluids and pass through without effect.

The toughness of the nylon provides the strong chewing resistance needed for important jaw exercise and effective help for the teething functions—but there is no tooth wear because nylon is non-abrasive. Being inert, nylon does not support the growth of microorganisms—and it can be washed in soap and water, or it can be sterilized by boiling or in an autoclave.

Nylabone® is highly recommended by veterinarians as a safe, healthy nylon bone that can't splinter or chip. Instead, Nylabone is frizzled by the dog's chewing action, creating a toothbrush-like surface that cleanses the teeth and massages the gums. Nylabone® and Nylaball®, the only chew products made of flavor-impregnated solid nylon, are available in your local pet shop.

Nothing, however, substitutes for periodic professional attention to your dog's teeth and gums, not any more than your toothbrush can do that for you. Have your dog's teeth cleaned by your veterinarian at least once a year, twice a year is better—and he will be healthier, happier and far more pleasant to live with.

Dogs with gum disease find chewing on Nylabone® to be uncomfortable and they may reject it. Remember: Nylabone® is a **pacifier** and is meant to substitute for shoes, furniture and table legs when your dog needs to chew. Nylabone® is NOT A TOY. But there is a very fine chew toy on the petshop shelf called GUMABONE®. This is made in the same shapes as Nylabone® but it is soft, semi-transparent, flexible and flavor-impregnated. Dogs love it once you have played with them for a few moments so they understand that it is a toy . . . and that it is theirs! These Gumabones® are even more indestructible than Nylabone®. *No dog should be without one.* They'll probably last for many years if you get the correct size. As your puppy grows, so must the size of the Gumabone® change. If you can afford only one toy, Gumabone® should be your choice!

NOT A GIMMICK—

GUMABONE Is a Major Technical Breakthrough. It Will Replace Rubber and Vinyl Dog Toys!

5. OBEDIENCE TRAINING

WHEN TO START TRAINING

You should never begin *serious* obedience training before your dog is seven or eight months old. (Some animal psychologists state that puppies can begin training when seven weeks old, if certain techniques are followed. These techniques, however, are still experimental and should be left to the professional trainer.) While your dog is still in his early puppyhood, concentrate on winning his confidence so he will love and admire you. Basic training can be started at the age of three or four months. He should be taught to walk nicely on a leash, sit and lie down on command, and come when he is called.

YOUR PART IN TRAINING

You must patiently demonstrate to your dog what each word of command means. Guide him with your hands and the training leash, reassuring him with your voice, through whatever routine you are teaching him. Repeat the word associated with the act. Demonstrate again and again to give the dog a chance to make the connection in his mind.

Once he begins to get the idea, use the word of command without any physical guidance. Drill him. When he makes mistakes, correct him, kindly at first, more severely as his training progresses. Try not to lose your patience or become irritated, and never slap him with your hand or the leash during the training session. Withholding praise or rebuking him will make him feel bad enough.

When he does what you want, praise him lavishly with words and with pats. Don't continually reward with dog candy or treats in training. The dog that gets into the habit of performing for a treat will seldom be fully dependable when he can't smell or see one in the offing. When he carries out a command, even though his performance is slow or sloppy, praise him and he will perform more readily the next time.

THE TRAINING VOICE

When you start training your dog, use your training voice, giving commands in a firm, clear tone. Once you give a command, persist until it is obeyed, even if you have to pull the dog to obey you. He must learn that training is different from playing, that a command once given must be obeyed no matter what distractions are present. Remember that the tone and pitch of your voice, not loudness, are the qualities that will influence your dog most.

Be consistent in the use of words during training. Confine your commands to as few words as possible and never change them. It is best for only one person to carry on the dog's training, because different people will use different words and tactics that will confuse your dog. The dog who hears "come," "get over here," "hurry up," "here, Rex," and other commands when he is wanted will become totally confused.

TRAINING LESSONS

Training is hard on the dog and the trainer. A young dog just cannot take more than ten minutes of training at a stretch, so limit the length of your first lessons. Then you can gradually increase the length of time to about thirty minutes. You'll find that you too will tend to become impatient when you stretch out a training lesson. If you find yourself losing your temper, stop and resume the lesson at another time. Before and after each lesson have a play period, but don't play during a training session. Even the youngest dog soon learns that schooling is a serious matter; fun comes afterward.

Don't spend too much time on one phase of training, or the dog will become bored. Always try to end a lesson on a pleasant note. Actually, in nine cases out of ten, if your dog isn't doing what you want it's because you're not getting the idea over to him properly.

YOUR TRAINING EQUIPMENT AND ITS USE

The leash is more properly called the lead, so we'll use that term here. The best leads for training are the six-foot webbed-cloth leads, usually olive-drab in color, and the six-foot leather lead. Fancier leads are available and may be used if desired.

You'll need a choke collar, consisting of a fabric (usually nylon) or a metal chain with rings on each end. Even though the name may sound frightening, it won't hurt your dog, and it is an absolute MUST in training. There is a right and a wrong way to put the training collar on. It should go around the dog's neck so that you can attach the lead to the ring at the end of the collar which passes over, not under the neck. It is most important that the collar is put on properly so it will tighten when the lead is pulled and ease when you relax your grip.

The correct way to hold the lead is also very important, as the collar should have some slack in it at all times, except when correcting. Holding the loop in your right hand, extend your arm out to the side, even with your shoulder. With your left hand, grasp the lead as close as possible to the collar, without making it tight. The remaining portion of the lead can

Your local pet store is the source of a large selection of leads and collars that can be used for training or showing, or just taking your pet for a walk. Since puppies quickly outgrow their first collars and leads, plan to purchase at least two sets of equipment.

be made into a loop which is held in the right hand. Keep this arm close to your body. Most corrections will be made with the left hand by giving the lead a jerk in the direction you want the dog to go.

HEELING

"Heeling" in dog language means having your dog walk alongside you on your left side, close to your leg, on lead or off. With patience and effort you can train your dog to walk with you even on a crowded street or in the presence of other dogs.

Now that you have learned the correct way to put on your dog's collar and how to hold the lead, you are ready to start with his first lesson in heeling. Make the dog sit at your left side. Using the dog's name and the command "Heel," start forward on your LEFT foot, giving a tug on the lead to get the dog started. Always use the dog's name first, followed by the command, such as "Rex, heel." Saying his name will help get his attention and will let him know that you are about to give a command.

Walk briskly, with even steps, going around in a large circle, square or straight line. While walking, make sure that your dog stays on the left side and close to your leg. If he lags behind, snap gently on the lead to get him up to you, then praise him lavishly for doing well. If he forges ahead or swings wide, stop and jerk the lead sharply and bring him back to the proper position. Always praise him when he returns to the correct place. As soon as you have snapped the lead to correct your dog, let it go slack again at the desired length. Don't drag the dog or keep the lead taut as this will develop into a tug of war which is ineffective.

To keep your dog's attention, talk to him as you keep him in place. You can also do a series of fast about-turns, giving the lead a jerk as you turn. He will gradually learn that he must pay attention or be jerked to your side. You can vary the routine by changing speeds, doing turns, figure-eights, and by zig-zagging across the training area.

"HEEL" MEANS "SIT," TOO

To the dog, the command "Heel" will also mean that he has to sit in the heel position at your left side when you stop walking with no additional command from you. As you practice heeling, make him sit whenever you stop, at first using the word "Sit," then with no command at all. He'll soon get the idea and sit down when you stop and wait for the command "Heel" to start walking again.

TRAINING TO SIT

Training your dog to sit should be fairly easy. Stand him on your left side, holding the lead fairly short, and command him to "Sit." As you give the verbal command, pull up slightly with the lead and push his hindquarters down. Do not let him lie down or stand up. If he does lie down, snap up on the lead until he rises to a sitting position again. If he is slow to respond, tug more sharply until he has done what you want him to. Keep him in a sitting position for a moment, then release the pressure on the lead and praise him. Constantly repeat the command as you hold him in a sitting position, thus fitting the word to the action in his mind. If he moves at all, immediately repeat the command and press him into a sitting position. After a time he will begin to get the idea and will sit without having to push his hindquarters down. When he reaches that stage, insist that he sit on command. Praise him often, always rewarding a correct action with your praise and affection.

THE "LIE DOWN" OR "DOWN"

The object of this is to get the dog to lie down either on the verbal command "Down" or when you give the hand signal, your hand raised in front of you, palm down. However, until the dog is really sure of the meaning of the command, and will do it by himself with no forcible action from you, the hand signal should only be used to accompany the verbal command. This command may be more difficult at first because it places the dog in a defenseless position, which may cause him to bolt away. Be lavish with your praise and affection when he has assumed the correct position and he will soon learn that nothing bad happens to him, and on the contrary will associate the "Down" position with pleasing his master or mistress.

Don't start training to lie down until the dog is almost letter-perfect in sitting on command. Place the dog in a sit, and kneel before him. With both hands, reach forward to his legs and take one front leg in each hand, thumbs up, holding just above the elbows. Lift his legs slightly off the ground and pull them somewhat out in front of him. Simultaneously, give the command "Down" and lower his front legs to the ground.

Hold the dog down and stroke him to let him know that staying down is what you want him to do. This method is far better than forcing a young dog down. Using force can cause him to become very frightened and he will begin to dislike any training. Always talk to your dog and let him know that you are very pleased with him, and soon you will find that you have a happy working dog.

After he begins to get the idea, slide the lead under your left foot and give the command "Down." At the same time, pull the lead. This will help get the dog down. Meanwhile, raise your hand in the down signal. Don't expect to accomplish all this in one session. Be patient and work with the dog. He'll cooperate if you show him just what you expect him to do.

THE "STAY"

The next step is to train your dog to stay either in a "Sit" or "Down" position. As before, use the lead to teach this command until your dog is responding perfectly to your instruction, then you may try it off the lead. To begin with the Sit-Stay, place your dog in a sitting position beside you in the automatic heel-sit position. Holding the leash in one hand (most trainers prefer the left), take a long step forward and turn to face him holding your free hand open, palm toward him, fingers pointing downward, in front of his nose and speak the command "Stay." If he offers to follow you, as it would be natural for him to do since this has been his ready position for heel, snap up on the lead to return him to the sit, put your hand in front of his face and repeat the command firmly once more. Allow him to remain sitting for a few seconds before going through the procedure again. Each time he successfully performs, praise him profusely and show him you are pleased with him.

Repeat this procedure until your dog behaves as if he understands what is expected of him. When he has mastered this procedure, step away to the right of him, then behind, then a few steps forward, a few steps to the side, and so on, until you have gone the full length of the leash. Anytime your dog offers to follow you, snap upward on the leash, extending your arm palm forward to him and repeat the command sharply. When he has demonstrated a willingness to remain in the correct position while you walk the full extent of the lead, you are ready to train him to remain in position using a longer length of cord, about 25 or 30 feet, and finally the Sit-Stay off the lead.

Once the Sit-Stay is learned, you can teach the Down-Stay by beginning with the Down command, then apply approximately the same methods as in the Sit-Stay.

THE COME ON COMMAND

You can train your dog to come when you call him if you begin when he is young. At first, work with him on lead. Sit the dog, then back away the length of the lead and call him, putting into your voice as much coaxing affection as possible. Give an easy tug on the lead to get him started. When he does come, make a big fuss over him—it might help at this point to give him a small piece of dog candy or food as a reward. He should get the idea soon. You can also move away from him the full length of the lead and call to him something like "Rex, come," then run backward a few steps and stop, making him sit directly in front of you.

Don't be too eager to practice coming on command off lead. Wait until you are certain that you have the dog under perfect control before you try calling him when he's free. Once he gets the idea that he can disobey a command and get away with it, your training program will suffer a serious setback. Keep in mind that your dog's life may depend on his immediate response to a command to come when he is called. If he disobeys off lead, put the lead back on and correct him severely with jerks of the lead.

TEACHING TO COME TO HEEL

The object of this is for you to stand still, say "Heel," and have your dog come right over to you and sit by your left knee in the heel position. If your dog has been trained to sit without command every time you stop, he's ready for this step.

Sit him in front of and facing you and step back one step. Moving only your left foot, pull the dog behind you, then step forward and pull him around until he is in a heel position. You can also have the dog go around by passing the lead behind your back. Use your left heel to straighten him out if he begins to sit behind you or crookedly. This may take a little work, but he will get the idea if you show him just what you want.

THE STAND

Your dog should be trained to stand in one spot without moving his feet, and he should allow a stranger to run his hand over his body and legs without showing any resentment or fear. Employ the same method you used in training him to stay on the sit and down. While walking, place your left hand out, palm toward his nose, and command him to stay. His first impulse will be to sit, so be prepared to stop him by placing your hand under his body, near his hindquarters, and holding him until he gets the idea that this is different from the command to sit. Praise him for standing, then walk to the end of the lead. Correct him strongly if he starts to move. Have a stranger approach him and run his hands over the dog's back and down his legs. Keep him standing until you come back to him. Walk around him from his left side, come to the heel position, and make sure that he does not sit until you command him to. This is a very valuable exercise. If you plan to show your dog, he will have to learn to stand in a show pose and allow the judge to examine him. The judge will run his hands along the dog's back and down the legs, so it is important that the dog stands calmly and steadfastly.

TRAINING SCHOOLS AND CLASSES

There are dog training schools in all parts of the country, some sponsored by the local humane society.

If you feel that you lack the time or the skill to train your dog yourself, there are professional dog trainers who will do it for you, but basically dog training is a matter of training YOU and your dog to work together as a team, and if you don't do it yourself you will miss a lot of fun. Don't give up after trying unsuccessfully for a short time. Try a little harder and you and your dog will be able to work things out.

ADVANCED TRAINING AND OBEDIENCE TRIALS

Once you begin training your dog and you see how well he does, you'll probably be bitten by the "obedience bug"—the desire to enter him in obedience trials held under American Kennel Club auspices.

The A.K.C. obedience trials are divided into three classes: Novice, Open and Utility.

In trials for advanced obedience degrees, your dog will have to successfully accomplish two scent discrimination exercises. From among several objects like the ones above, he will have to choose the one that has been touched by his handler or owner and carries that person's scent.

In the Novice Class the dog will be judged on the following basis:

TEST MAXIMUM SCORE

Heel on lead	40
Stand for examination	30
Heel free—off lead	40
Recall (come on command)	30
One-minute sit (handler in ring)	30
Three-minute down (handler in ring)	30
Maximum total score	200

If the dog "qualifies" in three shows by earning at least 50% of the points for each test, with a total of at least 170 for the trial, he has earned the Companion Dog degree and the letters C.D. (Companion Dog) are entered after his name in the American Kennel Club records.

The hurdle is used in different events in advanced obedience competition. It figures in the single jump, in the retrieve, and in the directed jump. The bar is adjustable, so that the height a dog must jump to successfully accomplish the particular exercise will be proportional to his size. Informal hurdles can be simulated out of a variety of different items for backyard or indoor practice before the actual trial.

After the dog has earned his Companion Dog title, he is eligible to enter the Open Class competition and compete for his next degree. He will be judged on this basis:

TEST MAXIMUM SCORE

Heel free 40
Drop on recall 30
Retrieve (wooden dumbbell) on flat 20
Retrieve over obstacle (hurdle) 30
Broad jump 20
Three-minute sit (handler out of ring) 30
Five-minute down (handler out of ring) 30
Maximum total score 200

Again he must qualify in three shows for the C.D.X. (Companion Dog Excellent) title, earning at least 50% of the points for each test, with a total of at least 170 for the trial. He is then eligible to compete in the Utility Class, where he can earn the Utility Dog (U.D.) degree in these rugged tests:

TEST MAXIMUM SCORE

Scent discrimination (picking up article handled by master
from group) Article 1 30
Scent discrimination Article 2 30
Directed Retrieve 30
Signal exercise (heeling, etc., on hand signal) 40
Directed jumping (over hurdle and bar jump) 40
Group examination 30
Maximum total score 200

For more complete information about these obedience trials, write for the American Kennel Club's *Regulations and Standards for Obedience Trials*. Dogs that are disqualified from breed shows because of neutering or physical defects are eligible to compete in these trials. Besides the formal A.K.C. obedience trials, there are informal "match" trials in which dogs compete for ribbons and inexpensive trophies. These shows are run by many local fanciers' clubs and by all-breed obedience clubs. In many localities the humane society and other groups conduct their own obedience shows. Your local newspaper, pet shop proprietor or kennel club can keep you informed about such shows in your vicinity, and you will find them listed in the different dog magazines or in the pet column of your paper.

6. BREEDING YOUR DOG

THE QUESTION OF SPAYING

If you feel that you will never want to raise a litter of purebred puppies, and if you do not wish to risk the possibility of an undesirable mating and surplus mongrel puppies inevitably destined for euthanasia at the local pound, you may want to have your female spayed. Spaying is generally best performed after the female has passed her first heat and before her first birthday; this allows the female to attain the normal female characteristics, while still being young enough to avoid the possible complications encountered when an older female is spayed. A spayed female will remain a healthy, lively pet. You often hear that an altered female will become very fat. However, if you cut down on her food intake, she will not gain weight.

On the other hand, if you wish to show your dog in American Kennel Club competition (altered females are disqualified) or enjoy the excitement and feeling of accomplishment of breeding and raising a litter of quality puppies, particularly in your breed and from your pet, then do not spay your dog until a more appropriate time.

Male dogs are almost never altered (castrated) unless they exhibit excessive sexual tendencies.

SEXUAL PHYSIOLOGY

Females usually reach sexual maturity (indicated by the first heat cycle, or season) at eight or nine months of age, but sexual maturity may occur as early as six months or as late as thirteen months of age. Generally, the larger the breed is the longer it takes to reach full maturity.

The average heat cycle (estrus period) lasts for twenty or twenty-one days, and occurs approximately every six months. For about five days immediately preceeding the heat period, the female generally displays restlessness and an increased appetite. The vulva, or external genitals, begins to swell. The discharge, which is bright red at the onset and gradually becomes pale pink to straw in color, increases in quantity for several days and then slowly subsides, finally ceasing altogether. The vaginal discharge is subject to much variation; in some bitches it is quite heavy, in others it may never appear, and in some it may be so slight as to go unnoticed.

About eight or nine days after the first appearance of the discharge, the female becomes very playful with other dogs, but will not allow a mating

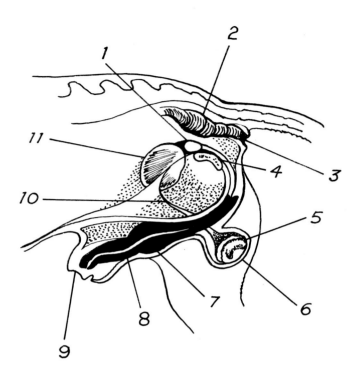

Reproductive system of a male dog: 1. Prostate 2. Rectum 3. Anus 4. Section of pelvic bone 5. Testicle 6. Scrotum 7. Bulb (part of Penis) 8. Penis 9. Sheath 10. Vas deferens 11. Bladder.

to take place. Anywhere from the tenth or eleventh day to the seventeenth or eighteenth day, the female will accept males and be able to conceive. Many biologists apply the term "heat" only to this receptive phase rather than to the whole estrus period, as is commonly done by dog fanciers.

The ova (egg cells) from the female's ovaries are discharged into the oviduct toward the close of the acceptance phase, usually the sixteenth to eighteenth day. From the eighteenth day until the end of the cycle, the female is still attractive to males, but she will repulse their advances. The entire estrus, however, may be quite variable; in some females vaginal bleeding ends and mating begins on the fourth day; in others the discharge may continue throughout the entire cycle and the female will not accept males until the seventeenth day or even later.

The male dog—simply referred to by fanciers as the "dog" or "stud," in contrast to the female, which is referred to as the "bitch"—upon reaching sexual maturity, usually at about six to eight months, is able,

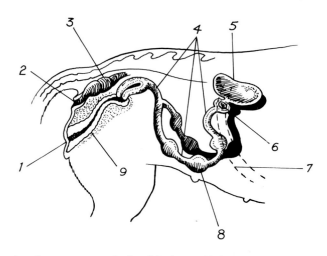

Reproductive system of the bitch: 1. Vulva 2. Anus 3. Rectum 4. Uterus 5. Kidney 6. Ovary 7. Ribs (indicated) 8. Developing embryo 9. Vagina.

like other domesticated mammals, to breed at any time throughout the year.

The testes, the sperm-producing organs of the male, descend from the body cavity into the scrotum at birth. The condition of cryptorchidism refers to the retention of one or both testes within the body cavity. A testicle retained within the body cavity is in an environment too hot for it to function normally. A retained testicle may also become cancerous. If only one testicle descends, the dog is known as a monorchid; if neither descends, the dog is known as an anorchid (dog fanciers, however, refer to a dog with the latter condition as a cryptorchid). A monorchid dog is a fertile animal; an anorchid is sterile.

The male dog's penis has a bulbous enlargement at its base and, in addition, like the penis of a number of other mammals, contains a bone. When mating occurs, pressure on the penis causes a reflex action that fills the bulb with blood, swelling it to five times its normal size within the female. This locks, or ties, the two animals together. After ejaculation, the animals usually remain tied for fifteen to thirty minutes. However, they may separate very quickly or remain together an hour or more, depending on the length of time for the blood to drain from the bulb.

CARE OF THE FEMALE IN ESTRUS

If you have a dog-proof run within your yard, it will be safe to leave your female in season there; if you don't have such a run, she should be shut indoors. Don't leave her alone outside even for a minute; she should be exercised only on lead. If you want to prevent the neighborhood dogs from congregating around your doorstep, as they inevitably will as soon as they discover that your female is in season, take her some distance from the house before you let her relieve herself. Take her in your car to a park or field for a chance to "stretch" her legs (always on lead, of course). Keep watch for male dogs, and if one approaches take the female back to the car. After the three weeks are up you can let her out as before with no worry that she can have puppies until her next season.

Some owners find it simpler to board their female at a kennel until her season is over. However, it really is not difficult to watch your female at home. There are various products on the market which are useful at this time. Although the female in season keeps herself quite clean, sometimes she unavoidably stains furniture or rugs. You can buy sanitary belts made expecially for dogs at your pet shop. Consult your veterinarian for information on pills to be taken to check odor during this period. There also is a pill that prevents the female from coming in season for extended periods, and there are many different types of liquids, powders and sprays of varying efficiency used to keep male dogs away. However, the

There are several products on the market designed to make life easier for both you and your bitch during the estrus cycle. Sanitary pads for dogs are one of these items and come complete with a belt for holding the pad in place.

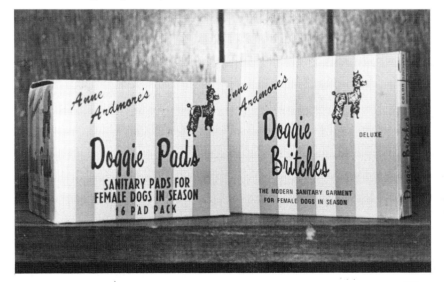

one safe rule (whatever products you use) is: keep your bitch away from dogs that could mount her.

SHOULD YOU BREED YOUR MALE?

Deciding whether or not to use a male dog as a stud is a question with two sides. The arguments for and against using a dog as a stud are often very close to ridiculous. A classic example would be the tale that once you use a dog as a stud he will lose his value as a show dog or any one of the other functions a dog may have. A sound rule may well be: if you have a stud who has proven his worth at the shows, place his services out for hire, if only for the betterment of the breed; if your dog is not of show quality, do not use him as a stud.

Top champion studs can bring their owners many dollars in breeding revenue. If the stud is as good as you feel he is, his services will soon be in great demand. Using a dog as a stud will not lower his value in other functions in any way. Many breeders will permit a male dog to breed an experienced female once, when about a year old, and then they begin to show their stud until he has gained his conformation championship. He is then placed out for hire through advertising in the various bulletins, journals and show catalogues, and through the stud registers maintained by many pet shops and kennel clubs.

SHOULD YOU BREED YOUR FEMALE?

If you are an amateur and decide to breed your female it would be wise to talk with a breeder and find out all that breeding and caring for puppies entails. You must be prepared to assume the responsibility of caring for the mother through her pregnancy and for the puppies until they are of saleable age. Raising a litter of puppies can be a rewarding experience, but it means work as well as fun, and there is no guarantee of financial profit. As the puppies grow older and require more room and care, the amateur breeder, in desperation, often sells the puppies for much less than they are worth; sometimes he has to give them away. If the cost of keeping the puppies will drain your finances, think twice.

If you have given careful consideration to all these things and still want to breed your female, remember that there is some preparation necessary before taking this step.

WHEN TO BREED

It is usually best to breed in the second or third season of your bitch. Consider when the puppies will be born and whether their birth and later care will interfere with your work or vacation plans. Gestation period is approximately fifty-eight to sixty-five days. Allow enough time to select

NORMAL BITCH MATING CYCLE

DISCHARGE BRIGHT RED, GRADUALLY TURNING PINK, THEN CREAM COLORED

PLAYFUL WITH DOGS

WILL ACCEPT STUD DURING THIS PERIOD

FOLLICLES DEVELOPING
TOWARD SURFACE OF OVARIES

VULVA SWELLS
APPETITE INCREASES
RESTLESSNESS

REPRODUCTIVE SYSTEM BECOMING CONGESTED

OVULATION PERIOD
OVA MOVING DOWN TUBES

WILL NOT ACCEPT STUD

REMAINDER OF HALF YEAR . . . 158 DAYS

the right stud for her. Don't be in a position of having to settle for any available stud if she comes into season sooner than expected. Your female will probably be ready to breed twelve days after the first colored discharge. You can usually make arrangements to board her with the owner of the male for a few days to insure her being there at the proper time, or you can take her to be mated and bring her home the same day. If she still appears receptive she may be bred again a day or two later. Some females never show signs of willingness, so it helps to have the experience of a breeder. The second day after the discharge changes color is the proper time; she may be bred for about three days following. For an additional week or so she may have some discharge and attract other dogs by her odor, but she can seldom be bred at this time.

HOW TO SELECT A STUD

Choose a mate for your female with an eye to countering her deficiencies. If possible, both male and female should have several ancestors in common within the last two or three generations, as such combinations generally "click" best. The male should have a good show record himself or be the sire of champions. The owner of the stud usually charges a fee for the use of the dog. The fee varies. Payment of a fee does not guarantee a litter, but it does generally confer the right to breed your female again to the stud if she does not have puppies the first time. In some cases the owner of the stud will agree to take a choice puppy in place of the stud fee. You and the owner of the stud should settle all details beforehand, including such questions as what age the puppies should reach before the

Maintenance of a state of excellent health is essential if you are contemplating breeding your bitch or stud. Poor health may not only interfere with reproductive processes but can actually rob your dog of his or her interest in mating. If you are not confident in commercial preparations, consult your vet for the best vitamin supplements to add to your dog's diet.

stud's owner can make his choice, what disposition is made of the single surviving puppy under an agreement by which the stud owner has the pick of the litter, and so on. In all cases, it is best that all agreements entered into by bitch owner and stud owner be in the form of a written contract.

It is customary for the female to be sent to the male. If the stud dog of your choice lives any distance from you, you will have to make arrangements to have your female shipped to him. The quickest way is by air, and if you call your nearest airport the airline people will give you information as to the best and fastest flight. Some airlines furnish their own crates for shipping, whereas others require that you furnish your own. The owner of the stud will make the arrangements for shipping the female back to you. You have to pay all shipping charges.

PREPARATION FOR BREEDING

Before you breed your female, make sure she is in good health. She should be neither too thin nor too fat. Skin diseases must be cured before breeding; a bitch with skin diseases can pass them on to her puppies. If

Perpetual Whelping Chart

	1	2	3	4	5	6	7	8	9	10	11	12	13	14	15	16	17	18	19	20	21	22	23	24	25	26	27	28	29	30	31
Bred—Jan.	1	2	3	4	5	6	7	8	9	10	11	12	13	14	15	16	17	18	19	20	21	22	23	24	25	26	27	28	29	30	31
Due—March	5	6	7	8	9	10	11	12	13	14	15	16	17	18	19	20	21	22	23	24	25	26	27	28	29	30	31	1	2	3	4
Bred—Feb.	1	2	3	4	5	6	7	8	9	10	11	12	13	14	15	16	17	18	19	20	21	22	23	24	25	26	27	28			
Due—April	5	6	7	8	9	10	11	12	13	14	15	16	17	18	19	20	21	22	23	24	25	26	27	28	29	30	1	2			
Bred—Mar.	1	2	3	4	5	6	7	8	9	10	11	12	13	14	15	16	17	18	19	20	21	22	23	24	25	26	27	28	29	30	31
Due—May	3	4	5	6	7	8	9	10	11	12	13	14	15	16	17	18	19	20	21	22	23	24	25	26	27	28	29	30	31	1	2
Bred—Apr.	1	2	3	4	5	6	7	8	9	10	11	12	13	14	15	16	17	18	19	20	21	22	23	24	25	26	27	28	29	30	
Due—June	3	4	5	6	7	8	9	10	11	12	13	14	15	16	17	18	19	20	21	22	23	24	25	26	27	28	29	30	1	2	
Bred—May	1	2	3	4	5	6	7	8	9	10	11	12	13	14	15	16	17	18	19	20	21	22	23	24	25	26	27	28	29	30	31
Due—July	3	4	5	6	7	8	9	10	11	12	13	14	15	16	17	18	19	20	21	22	23	24	25	26	27	28	29	30	31	1	2
Bred—June	1	2	3	4	5	6	7	8	9	10	11	12	13	14	15	16	17	18	19	20	21	22	23	24	25	26	27	28	29	30	
Due—August	3	4	5	6	7	8	9	10	11	12	13	14	15	16	17	18	19	20	21	22	23	24	25	26	27	28	29	30	31	1	
Bred—July	1	2	3	4	5	6	7	8	9	10	11	12	13	14	15	16	17	18	19	20	21	22	23	24	25	26	27	28	29	30	31
Due—September	2	3	4	5	6	7	8	9	10	11	12	13	14	15	16	17	18	19	20	21	22	23	24	25	26	27	28	29	30	1	2
Bred—Aug.	1	2	3	4	5	6	7	8	9	10	11	12	13	14	15	16	17	18	19	20	21	22	23	24	25	26	27	28	29	30	31
Due—October	3	4	5	6	7	8	9	10	11	12	13	14	15	16	17	18	19	20	21	22	23	24	25	26	27	28	29	30	31	1	2
Bred—Sept.	1	2	3	4	5	6	7	8	9	10	11	12	13	14	15	16	17	18	19	20	21	22	23	24	25	26	27	28	29	30	
Due—November	3	4	5	6	7	8	9	10	11	12	13	14	15	16	17	18	19	20	21	22	23	24	25	26	27	28	29	30	1	2	
Bred—Oct.	1	2	3	4	5	6	7	8	9	10	11	12	13	14	15	16	17	18	19	20	21	22	23	24	25	26	27	28	29	30	31
Due—December	3	4	5	6	7	8	9	10	11	12	13	14	15	16	17	18	19	20	21	22	23	24	25	26	27	28	29	30	31	1	2
Bred—Nov.	1	2	3	4	5	6	7	8	9	10	11	12	13	14	15	16	17	18	19	20	21	22	23	24	25	26	27	28	29	30	
Due—January	3	4	5	6	7	8	9	10	11	12	13	14	15	16	17	18	19	20	21	22	23	24	25	26	27	28	29	30	31	1	
Bred—Dec.	1	2	3	4	5	6	7	8	9	10	11	12	13	14	15	16	17	18	19	20	21	22	23	24	25	26	27	28	29	30	31
Due—February	2	3	4	5	6	7	8	9	10	11	12	13	14	15	16	17	18	19	20	21	22	23	24	25	26	27	28	1	2	3	4

Overflow (next-month due dates) on the right side of the chart:

Bred days	Due
28 29 30 31	April 1 2 3 4
27 28	May 1 2
30 31	June 1 2
29 30	July 1 2
30 31	August 1 2
30	Sept. 1
30 31	Oct. 1 2
30 31	Nov. 1 2
29 30	Dec. 1 2
30 31	Jan. 1 2
30	Feb. 1
28 29 30 31	March 1 2 3 4

she has worms she should be wormed before being bred, or within three weeks afterward. It is a good idea to have your veterinarian give her a booster shot for distemper and hepatitis before the puppies are born. This will increase the immunity the puppies receive during their early, most vulnerable period. Choose a dependable veterinarian and rely on him if there is an emergency when your female whelps.

Do not breed your bitch after she reaches six years of age. If you wish to breed her several times while she is young, it is wise to breed her only once a year. In other words, breed her, skip at least one season, and then breed her again. This will allow her to gain back her full strength between whelpings.

THE IMPORTANCE AND APPLICATION OF GENETICS

Any person attempting to breed dogs should have a basic understanding of the transmission of traits, or characteristics, from the parents to the offspring and some familiarity with the more widely used genetic terms that he will probably encounter. A knowledge of the fundamental mechanics of genetics enables a breeder to better comprehend the passing on of good traits and bad from generation to generation and how a stud and bitch either complement or detract from each other's traits. It enables him to make a more judicial and scientific decision in selecting potential mates.

Inheritance, fundamentally, is due to the existence of microscopic units, known as *GENES*, present in the cells of all individuals. Genes somehow control the biochemical reactions that occur within the embryo or adult organism. This control results in changing or guiding the development of the organism's characteristics. A "string" of attached genes is known as a *CHROMOSOME*. With a few important exceptions, every chromosome has a partner chromosome carrying a duplicate or equivalent set of genes. Each gene, therefore, has a partner gene, known as an *ALLELE*. The number of different pairs of chromosomes present in the cells of the organism varies with the type of organism; a certain parasitic worm has only one pair, a certain fruit fly has four different pairs, man has 23 different pairs and your dog has 39 different pairs per cell. Because each chromosome may have many hundreds of genes, a single cell of the body may contain a total of several thousand genes. Heredity is obviously a very complex matter.

In the simplest form of genetic inheritance, one particular gene and its duplicate, or allele, on the partner chromosome control a single characteristic. The presence of freckles in the human skin, for example, is believed to be due to the influence of a single pair of genes.

Each cell of the body contains the specific number of paired

FERTILIZATION

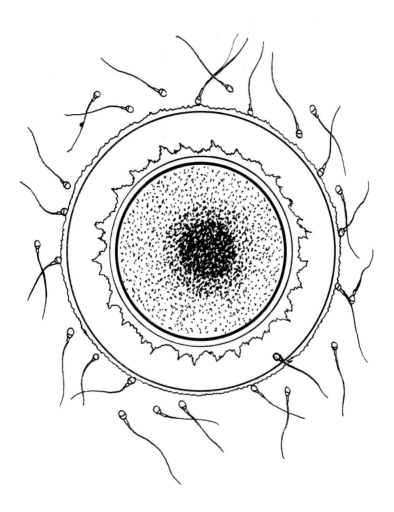

An egg, a special giant cell which the female ovaries produce, is being assaulted by sperm which are attempting to pierce the outer layer of the cell. Only one sperm cell penetration is necessary for fertilization. The first sperm to enter and reach the nucleus will bring with it the necessary chromosomes which will unite with those of the egg. With this union, the full complement of chromosomes necessary for the creation of a new fetus is complete. No other sperm cells are now able to penetrate the egg.

chromosomes characteristic of the organism. Because each type of gene is present on both chromosomes of a chromosome pair, each type of gene is therefore present in duplicate. The fusion of a sperm cell from the male with an egg cell from the female, as occurs in fertilization, should therefore result in offspring having a quadruplicate number (4) of each type of gene. Mating of these individuals would then produce progeny having an octuplicate number (8) of each type of gene, and so on. This, however, is normally prevented by a special process. When ordinary body cells prepare to divide to form more tissue, each pair of chromosomes duplicates itself so that there are four partner chromosomes of each kind instead of only two. When the cell divides, two of the four partners, or one pair, go into each new cell. This process, known as *MITOSIS,* insures that each new body cell contains the proper number of chromosomes. Reproductive cells (sperm and egg cells), however, undergo a special kind of division known as *MEIOSIS.* In meiosis, the chromosome pairs do not duplicate themselves, and thus when the reproductive cells reach the final dividing stage only one chromosome, or one-half of the pair, goes into each new reproductive cell. Each reproductive cell, therefore, has only half the normal number of chromosomes. These are referred to as *HAPLOID* cells, in contrast to *DIPLOID* cells, which have the full number of chromosomes. When the haploid sperm cell fuses with the haploid egg cell in fertilization, the resulting offspring has the normal diploid number of chromosomes.

If both partner genes, or alleles, affect the trait in an identical manner, the genes are said to be *HOMOZYGOUS,* but if one affects the character in a manner different from the other gene, or allele, the genes are said to be *HETEROZYGOUS.* For example, in the pair of genes affecting eye color in humans, if each gene of the pair produces blue eyes, while the other gene, or allele, produces brown eyes, they are said to be heterozygous. The presence of heterozygous genes raises the question, "Will the offspring have blue eyes or brown eyes?" which in turn introduces another genetic principle.

DOMINANCE and RECESSIVENESS

If one gene of a pair can block the action of its partner, or allele, while still producing its own effect, that gene is said to be dominant over its allele. Its allele, on the other hand, is said to be recessive. In the case of heterozygous genes for eye color, the brown eye gene is dominant over the recessive blue eye gene, and the offspring therefore will have brown eyes. Much less common is the occurrence of gene pairs in which neither gene is completely dominant over the other. This, known as IN-COMPLETE or PARTIAL DOMINANCE, results in a blending of the

74

| SIRE and DAM | PROGENY |

MENDELIAN EXPECTATION CHART

Pictured are the six possible ways in which a pair of genes can unite. The white boxes represent dominant genes; the black boxes represent recessives. Half of the genes of the sire will unite with half of the genes of the dam, and the expected results of such a mating are shown in the progeny combinations. Ratios apply to expectancy over large litters, except in lines 1, 2 and 6 where expectancy is realized in every litter (the exception due to mutation).

opposing influences. In cattle, if a homozygous (pure) red bull is mated with a homozygous (pure) white cow, the calf will be roan, a blending of red and white hairs in its coat, rather than either all red or all white.

During meiosis, or division of the reproductive (sperm and egg) cells, each pair of chromosomes splits, and one-half of each pair goes into one of the two new cells. Thus, in the case of eye color genes, one new reproductive cell will get the chromosome carrying the blue eye gene, while the other new reproductive cell will get the chromosome carrying the brown eye gene, and so on for each pair of chromosomes. If an organism has only one pair of chromosomes—called pair A, made up of chromosomes A_1 and A_2, and pair B, made up of chromosomes B_1 and B_2—each new reproductive cell will get one chromosome from each pair, and four different combinations are possible: A_1 and B_1; A_1 and B_2; A_2 and B_1; or A_2 and B_2. If the blue eye gene is on A_1, the brown eye gene on A_2, and the gene for curly hair on B_1, and the gene for straight hair on B_2, each of the above combinations will exert a different genetic effect on the offspring. This different grouping of chromosomes in the new reproductive cell as a result of meiotic cell division is known as *INDEPENDENT ASSORTMENT* and is one reason why variation occurs in the offspring. In the dog, with 39 pairs of chromosomes, the possibilites of variation through independent assortment are tremendous.

But variation does not end here. For example, if two dominant genes, such as the genes for brown eyes and dark hair, were on the same chromosome, all brown-eyed people would have dark hair. Yet in instances where such joined or *LINKED* genes do occur, the two characteristics do not always appear together in the same offspring. This is due to a process known as a *CROSS-OVER* or *RECOMBINATION*. Recombination is the mutual exchange of corresponding blocks of genes between the two chromosomes in a pair. That is, during cell division, the two chromosomes may exchange their tip sections or other corresponding segments. If the segments exchanged contain the eye color genes, the brown eye gene will be transferred from the chromosome carrying the dark hair gene to the chromosome carrying the light hair gene, and then brown eyes will occur with light hair, provided that the individual is homozygous for the recessive light hair gene.

Another important source of variation is *MUTATION*. In mutation, a gene becomes altered, such as by exposure to irradiation, and exerts a different effect than it did before. Most mutations are harmful to the organism, and some may result in death. Offspring carrying mutated genes and showing the effects of these mutations are known as *MUTANTS* or *SPORTS*. Mutation also means that instead of only two alleles for eye color, such as brown and blue, there may now be three or more (gray, black, etc.) creating a much larger source for possible variation in the offspring.

Further complications in the transmission and appearance of genetic traits are the phenomena known as *EPISTATIS* and *PLEIOTROPY*. Epistatis refers to a gene exerting influence on genes other than its own allele. In all-white red-eyed (albino) guinea pigs, for example, the gene controlling intensity of color is epistatic to any other color gene and prevents that gene from producing its effect. Thus, even if a gene for red spots were present in the cells of the guinea pig, the color intensity gene would prevent the red spots from appearing in the guinea pig's white coat. *Pleiotropy* refers to the fact that a single gene may control a number of characteristics. In the fruit fly, for example, the gene that controls eye color may also affect the structure of certain body parts and even the lifespan of the insect.

One special pair of chromosomes is known as the sex chromosomes. In man, dog, and other mammals, these chromosomes are of two types, designated as X and Y. Under normal conditions, a mammal carrying one X-type and one Y-type is a male. Females have two X chromosomes and can only contribute X chromosomes to the offspring, but the male can contribute either an X or a Y.

If the male's sperm carrying an X chromosome fertilizes the female's egg cell (X), the offspring (XX) will be a female; if a sperm carrying a Y chromosome fertilizes the egg (X), the offspring (XY) will be male. It is the male, therefore, that determines the sex of the offspring in mammals.

Traits controlled by genes present on the sex chromosome, and which appear in only one sex, are said to be *SEX LINKED*. If, for example, a rare recessive gene occurs on the X chromosome, it cannot exert its effect in the female because the dominant allele on the other X chromosomes will counteract it. In the male, however, there is no second X chromosome, and if the Y chromosome cannot offer any countereffect, the recessive character will appear. There are also *SEX-LIMITED* characteristics: these appear primarily or solely in one sex, but the genes for these traits are not carried on the sex chromosomes. Sex-limited traits appear when genes on other chromosomes exert their effect in the proper hormonal (male or female) environment. Sex-linked and sex-limited transmission is how a trait may skip a generation, by being passed from grandfather to grandson through a mother in which the trait, though present, does not show.

In dealing with the simplest form of heredity—one gene effecting one character—there is an expected ratio of the offspring displaying the character to those who do not display it, depending upon the genetic makeup of the parents. If a parent is homozygous for a character, such as blue eyes, it makes no difference which half of the chromosome pair enters the new reproductive cell, because each chromosome carries the gene for blue eyes. If a parent is heterozygous, however, one reproductive cell will receive the brown eye gene while the other will receive the blue eye gene. If both parents are homozygous for blue eyes, all the offspring will receive two blue eye genes, and all will have blue eyes. If a parent is homozygous for blue eyes, and the other parent is homozygous for brown eyes, all the offspring will be heterozygous, receiving one brown eye and one blue eye gene, and because brown is dominant, all will have brown eyes. If both parents are heterozygous, both the blue eye gene and the brown eye gene from one parent have an equal likelihood of ending up with either the blue eye or the brown eye gene from the other parent. This results in a ratio of two heterozygous offspring to the one homozygous for brown eyes and one homozygous for blue eyes, giving a total genetic, or genotypic, ratio of 2:1:1 or, as it is more commonly arranged, 1:2:1. As the two heterozygous as well as the homozygous brown eye offspring will have brown eyes, the ratio of brown eyes to blue eyes (or phenotypic ratio) will be 3:1.

If one parent is heterozygous and the other parent is homozygous for the recessive gene for blue eyes, half of the offspring will be homozygous for the recessive blue-eyed trait.

If the homozygous parent, however, has the dominant gene (brown eyes), half of the offspring will be heterozygous and half will be homozygous, as before, but all will have brown eyes. By repeated determinations of these ratios in the offspring, geneticists are able to analyze the genetic makeup of the parents.

Before leaving heredity, it might be well to explain the difference between inbreeding, outcrossing, line breeding, and similar terms. Basically, there are only inbreeding and outbreeding. Inbreeding, however, according to its intensity, is usually divided into interbreeding proper and line breeding. Inbreeding proper is considered to be the mating of very closely related individuals, generally within the immediate family, but this is sometimes extended to include matings to first cousins and grandparents. Line breeding is the mating of more distantly related animals, that is, animals not immediately related to each other but having a common ancestor, such as the same grandsire or great-grandsire. Outbreeding is divided into outcrossing, which is the mating of dogs from different families within the same breed, and cross-breeding, which is mating purebred dogs from different breeds.

From the foregoing discussion of genetics, it should be realized that the theory of telegony, which states that the sire of one litter can influence future litters sired by other studs, is simply not true; it is possible, however, if several males mate with a female during a single estrus cycle, that the various puppies in the litter may have different sires (but not two sires for any one puppy). It should also be realized that blood does not really enter into the transmission of inheritance, although people commonly speak of "bloodlines," "pure-blooded," etc.

7. CARE OF THE MOTHER AND THE NEW FAMILY

PRENATAL CARE OF THE FEMALE

You can expect the puppies nine weeks from the day of breeding, although 58 days is as common as 63. During this time the female should receive normal care and exercise. If she is overweight, don't increase her food at first; excess weight at whelping time is not good. If she is on the thin side, build her up, giving her a morning meal of cereal and egg yolk. Consult your veterinarian as to increasing her vitamins and mineral supplement. During the last weeks the puppies grow enormously, and the mother will have little room for food and less appetite. Divide her meals into smaller portions and feed her more often. If she loses her appetite, tempt her with meat, liver, chicken, etc.

As she grows heavier, eliminate violent exercise and jumping. Do not eliminate exercise entirely, as walking is beneficial to the female in whelp, and mild exercise will maintain her muscle tone in preparation for the birth. Weigh your female after breeding and keep a record of her weight each week thereafter. Groom your bitch daily—some females have a slight discharge during gestation, more prevalent during the last two weeks, so wash the vulva with warm water daily. Usually, by the end of the fifth week you can notice a broadening across her loins, and her breasts become firmer. By the end of the sixth week your veterinarian can tell you whether or not she is pregnant.

PREPARATION OF WHELPING QUARTERS

Prepare a whelping box a few days before the puppies are due, and allow the mother to sleep there overnight or to spend some time in it during the day to become accustomed to it. Then she is less likely to try to have her pups under the front porch or in the middle of your bed. The box should have a wooden floor. Sides about a foot high will keep the puppies in but enable the mother to get out after she has fed them. If the weather is cold, the box should be raised about an inch off the floor.

You should place a guard rail in the whelping box to prevent the mother from rolling over onto the pups and smothering them. This guard is a strip of wood which will project out and above the floor of the box, keeping the bitch from pressing up against the sides of the box.

GUARD RAIL

SIDE BOARDS - ADDED LATER

STEP

ONE SIDE HINGED
FOR EASY CLEANING

WHELPING BOX

Layers of newspaper spread over the whole area will make excellent bedding and be absorbent enough to keep the surface warm and dry. They should be removed daily and replaced with another thick layer. An old quilt or washable blanket makes better footing for the nursing puppies than slippery newspaper during the first week, and is softer for the mother. The quilt should be secured firmly.

SUPPLIES TO HAVE ON HAND

As soon as you have the whelping box prepared, set up the nursery by collecting the various supplies you will need when the puppies arrive. You should have the following items on hand: a box lined with towels for the puppies, a heating pad or hot water bottle to keep the puppy box warm, a pile of clean terrycloth towels or washcloths to remove membranes and to dry puppies, a stack of folded newspapers, a roll of paper towels, vaseline, rubber gloves, soap, iodine, muzzle, cotton balls, a small pair of blunt scissors to cut umbilical cords (place scissors into an open bottle of alcohol so they keep freshly sterilized), a rectal thermometer, white thread, a flashlight in case the electricity goes off, a waste container, and a scale for weighing each puppy at birth.

It is necessary that the whelping room be warm and free from drafts, because puppies are delivered wet from the mother. Keep a little notebook and pencil handy so you can record the duration of the first labor and the time between the arrival of each puppy. If there is trouble in whelping, this is the information that the veterinarian will want. Keep his telephone number handy in case you have to call him in an emergency, and warn him to be prepared for an emergency, should you need him.

WHELPING

Be prepared for the actual whelping several days in advance. Usually the female will tear up papers, try to dig nests, refuse food, and generally act restless and nervous. These may be false alarms; the real test is her temperature, which will drop to below 100°F about twelve hours before whelping. Take her temperature rectally at a set time each day, starting about a week before she is due to whelp. After her temperature goes down, keep her constantly with you or put her in the whelping box and stay in the room with her. She will seem anxious and look to you for reassurance. During the birth, if neccesary, be prepared to remove the membranes covering the puppy's head if the mother fails to do this, for the puppy could smother otherwise.

The mother should start licking the puppy as soon as it is out of the sac, thus drying and stimulating it, but if she does not perform this task you can do it with a rough towel, instead. The afterbirth should follow the birth of each puppy, attached to the puppy by the umbilical cord. Watch to make sure that each is expelled, for retaining this material can cause infection. The mother probably will eat the afterbirth after biting the cord. One or two will not hurt her; they stimulate milk supply as well as labor for remaining puppies. Too many, however, can make her lose her appetite for the food she needs to feed her puppies and regain her strength, so remove the rest of them along with the soiled newspaper, and keep the box dry and clean to relieve her anxiety.

If a puppy does not start breathing, wrap him in a towel, hold him upside down with his head toward the ground, and shake him vigorously. If he still does not breathe, rub his ribs briskly; if this also fails, administer artificial respiration by compressing his ribs about twenty times per minute.

If the mother does not bite the cord, or bites it too close to the body, you should take over the job to prevent an umbilical hernia. Cut the cord a short distance from the body with your blunt scissors. Put a drop of iodine on the end of the cord; it will dry up and fall off in a few days.

The puppies should follow each other at regular intervals, but deliveries can be as short as five minutes or as long as two hours apart. A puppy may be presented backwards; if the mother does not seem to be in trouble, *do not interfere.* But if enough of the puppy is outside the birth canal, use a rough towel and help her by pulling gently on the puppy.

Pull only when she pushes. A rear-first, or breech birth can cause a puppy to strangle on its own umbilical cord, so don't let the mother struggle too long. Breech birth is quite common.

When you think all the puppies have been whelped, have your veterinarian examine the mother to determine if all the afterbirths have been expelled. He will probably give her an injection to be certain that the uterus is clean, a shot of calcium for prevention of eclampsia, and possibly an injection of penicillin to prevent infection.

CAESAREAN SECTION

Sometimes a Caesarean section is necessary, although very rarely. The operation of removing the pups by cutting into the abdomen and uterus of the bitch is generally safe; however, if the emergency Caesarean section follows a prolonged, exhausting and fruitless labor, the danger to the bitch is substantially increased.

Reasons for resorting to a Caesarean section include: 1. dystocia due to an abnormally large pup, 2. one presenting in such a way that it cannot get out, is blocking the passage and birth of its littermates or is threatening the life of its dam, 3. an abnormal pelvis in the bitch which does not allow passage of the pups (such as a previous pelvic fracture), 4. inertia, 5. long and arduous labor which exhausts the bitch to the point where weakness causes the uterine and abdominal contractions to stop.

Your bitch can be operated on without losing consciousness if your veterinarian selects to operate with a hypnotic and local anesthesia. The local anesthesia is injected, the incision made, and the pups taken from the semi-conscious bitch.

Gas anesthesia is the safest type of general anesthetic for delivering pups; if barbiturate anesthetics are used intravenously, the puppies may be quite effected by these drugs as they pass through the placental barrier.

Regardless of which method is used for the Caesarean section, the patient should be kept in a warm, clean bed after surgery until she recovers from the anesthesia. The pups should not be placed with the dam until she is once again alert. If the pups are also depressed from the anesthetic, artificial respiration may be required. It is imperative that the pups be kept dry and warm following the delivery.

Offer the puppies to their mother one at a time. After she licks a pup, help it to get settled on a teat and observe them carefully. Rarely, the bitch may not accept her puppies, but this may only be a temporary situation. Watch the mother when she goes out to do her duties; her sutures (stitches) should not be subjected to any undue strain. A binder may interfere with emptying several breasts, but aside from this she will behave in a normal manner. The stitches will be removed in about two weeks and she will be as good as new.

In the cases of both normal and Caesarean delivery the female's temperature should be checked twice daily for one week after delivery. A temperature of over 102°F should be reported to your veterinarian and his directions followed to the letter.

ECLAMPSIA

Eclampsia, or "milk fever," is caused by a lowered calcium content of the blood, due to the bitch's depleting her body's calcium reserves for the production of milk. It is a word that has been fearsome in the dog-breeding world for many years. If it occurs after whelping, the puppies and the mother are in severe danger. Help must be given immediately. The female stiffens her legs, has pale gums, and is likely to have minor convulsions. Puppies must be taken from her and calcium and dextrose administered to her intravenously. However, this is a rare thing and the symptoms so obvious, that assuredly the owner's first thought is that something is wrong and that the veterinarian is needed at once. With proper nutrition during gestation and lactation, a lack of calcium is not to be expected. The best preventive medicine is to see that the female is parasite free, in good condition, and properly cared for from the day she is mated.

HOW TO TAKE CARE OF A LARGE LITTER

The size of a litter varies greatly. If your bitch has a large litter she may have trouble feeding all of the puppies. You can help her by preparing an extra puppy box. Leave half the litter with the mother and the other half in a warm place, changing their places at two-hour intervals at first. Later you may change them less frequently, leaving them all together except during the day. Try supplementary feeding, too, as soon as their eyes are open, since at about two weeks they will lap from a dish.

RAISING THE PUPPIES

Hold each puppy to a breast as soon as he is dry, for a good meal without competition. Then he may join his littermates in the basket, out of his mother's way, while she is whelping. Keep a supply of evaporated milk on hand for emergencies, or later weaning. A formula of evaporated milk, corn syrup and a little water with egg yolk should be warmed and fed in a doll or baby bottle if necessary. A supplementary feeding often helps weak pups over the hump. Keep track of birth weights and take weekly readings so you will have an accurate record of the pups' growth and health.

This compartmentalized incubator demonstrates one method of caring for orphaned puppies. Orphaned pups need to be kept warm by artificial means since they do not have their mother to cuddle next to.

After the puppies have arrived, take the mother outside for a walk and drink, and then leave her to take care of them. She will probably not want to stay away more than a minute or two for the first few weeks. Be sure to keep water available at all times, and feed her milk or broth frequently, as she needs liquids to produce milk. To encourage her to eat, offer her the foods she likes best, until she asks to be fed without your tempting her. She will soon develop a ravenous appetite and should have at least two large meals a day, with dry food available in addition.

Prepare a warm place to put the puppies after they are born to keep them dry and help them to a good start in life. Cover an electric heating pad or hot-water bottle with flannel and put it in the bottom of a cardboard box. Set the box near the mother so that she can see her puppies. She will usually allow you to help, but don't take the puppies out of sight, and let her handle things if your interference seems to make her nervous.

Be sure that all of the puppies are getting enough to eat. If the mother sits or stands, instead of lying still to nurse, the probable cause is scratching from the puppies's nails. You can remedy this by clipping them, as you do hers. Manicure scissors will do for these tiny claws.

The puppies should normally be completely weaned at six weeks, although you start to feed them at three weeks. They will find it easier to lap semi-solid food. At four weeks they will eat four meals a day, and soon do without their mother entirely. Start them on mixed dog food, or leave it with them in a dish for self-feeding. Don't leave water with them all the time; at this age everything is to play with and they will use it as a wading pool. They can drink all they need if it is offered several times a day, after meals.

As the puppies grow up the mother will go into the pen only to nurse them, first sitting up and then standing. To dry her up completely, keep the mother away for longer periods, and then completely. The little milk left will be reabsorbed.

AIRING THE PUPPIES

The puppies may be put outside, unless it is too cold, as soon as their eyes are open. They will benefit from the sunlight and the vitamin D it provides. A rubber mat or newspapers underneath will protect them from cold or damp.

WORMING

You can expect a litter of pups to need at least one worming before they are ready to go to new homes, so take a stool sample to your veterinarian at about six weeks of age. Also, the litter should receive their first temporary shots, which are usually distemper-hepatitis-leptospirosis globulin. Today many kennels are advised by veterinarians to administer these preventative shots even earlier than six weeks, and in special cases they may begin right after birth. The puppy derives immunity from his mother's milk during the first twenty-four hours of his life; this immunity lasts for a varying length of time. Some mothers do not offer any immunity to their young at all. Therefore, in a kennel where the exposure rate is high, and many dogs come and go to shows, and disease may easily be brought to the premises, prophylactic treatment must start early. In the average home, where there is one female and one litter, six weeks is the proper time to start this treatment, and it must be repeated every one to two weeks until the puppies are old enough to have their permanent shots.

PUPPY SOCIALIZATION

Animal psychologists, research scientists and people who train dogs to work closely with people, such as trainers of seeing-eye dogs, have found that the first few weeks of a puppy's life is a critical time. The treatment a puppy receives during this stage determines whether he will become a mentally stable, trustworthy dog that likes people and is able to fit into their particular lifestyle. In general, the dog that is to be a reliable show dog or loving pet must be cuddled often, and experience pleasurable associations with people from a very early age. It is the duty of every creditable breeder to be willing to commit the amount of time necessary to socialize his puppies before he decides to breed his bitch. The behavior of his puppies, whether they are show prospects or pets, reflects on the breed and on his kennel name, two very good reasons for giving the puppies the kind of exposure to human companionship that will turn them into desirable adult dogs. This is not to deny heredity, but to stress the importance of human association in the early weeks of a puppy's life.

Some experts feel that the first three weeks of a puppy's life are completely taken up with nursing, sleeping and keeping warm snuggling with his littermates and dam, and that people-geared socialization should begin after these first three weeks. Others feel that it should begin right away, but that the form varies with the age. During the first weeks while the puppy is still gaining strength and weight and until his eyes are open, socialization should consist of simply holding the tiny pup, stroking its back and tummy for a few minutes and then putting it back with its mother. This should take place with each puppy, every day. As the puppy grows older, the time can be lengthened.

When the puppies are old enough to start eating solid foods, you can reinforce the pleasure contact by feeding them by hand. Basic training and developing receptivity to further training when they are older takes place at this point, so when you call them to you for the hand-held food, always use the same catch phrase. When the puppies are about a month old it's time to reinforce their sense of self-sufficiency and ease in new surroundings. This will also ease the transition to a new home. Remove the pups from their whelping box, which until now has circumscribed nearly their entire world, and take them to a different scene. The pup with the most adaptable nature is the one who will immediately move about and begin to explore this new setting. Puppies that are frightened and do not relax after a short time in this new environment should be put back with their mates until next time.

When they are six weeks old, puppies can be further disposed to training by putting a collar on them so they will get used to the feeling of it. Then put on the leash, not to take them for a walk, but just to let them run around in it so they get used to the idea. Later, more serious training can take place by the new owner with the puppy that is taking his place as a temperamentally sound, self-assured, friendly youngster in the world of his human companions.

8. GENERAL HEALTH CARE

WATCHING YOUR PUPPY'S HEALTH

First, don't be frightened by the number of diseases a dog can contract. The majority of dogs never get any of them. Don't become a dog-hypochondriac. All dogs have days when they feel lazy and want to lie around doing nothing. For the few diseases that you might be concerned about, remember that your veterinarian is your dog's best friend. When you first get your puppy, select a veterinarian whom you have faith in. He will get to know your dog and will be glad to have you consult him for advice. A dog needs little medical care, but that little is essential to his good health and well-being. He needs:

1. Proper diet at regular hours
2. Clean, roomy housing
3. Daily exercise
4. Companionship and love
5. Frequent grooming
6. Regular check-ups by your veterinarian

THE USEFUL THERMOMETER

Almost every serious ailment shows itself by an increase in the dog's body temperature. If your dog acts lifeless, looks dull-eyed, and gives the impression of illness, check his temperature by using a rectal thermometer. A stubby end rectal thermometer of either plastic or glass is best suited for this procedure. Although uncommon, there is always the hazard of possible breakage should he become excited during insertion. However, he is easily calmed if you soothe him when the routine is taking place. Hold the dog securely, and insert the thermometer, which you have lubricated with vaseline, and take a reading. The average normal temperature for your dog will be 101.5 °F. Excitement may raise the temperature slightly, but any rise of more than a few points is cause for alarm, and your vet should be consulted.

EMERGENCY FIRST AID

In general, a dog will heal his wounds by licking them. If he swallows anything harmful, chances are that he will throw it up. But it will probably make you feel better to help him if he is hurt, so treat his wounds as you would your own. Wash out the dirt and apply an antiseptic.

If you fear that your dog has swallowed poison, get him to the veterinarian's *at once.* In the meantime, try and locate the source of poisoning; if he has swallowed, for example, a cleaning fluid kept in your house, check the bottle label to see if inducing the dog to vomit is necessary. In some cases, inducing the dog to vomit can be very harmful, depending upon the type of poison swallowed. Amateur diagnosis is very dangerous, when you consider that time is so extremely important.

Accidents

Accidents, unfortunately, will happen so it is best to be prepared. If your dog gets hit by a car, keep him absolutely quiet, move him as little as possible and get veterinary treatment as soon as possible. It is unwise to give any stimulants such as brandy or other alcoholic liquids where there is visible external hemorrhage or the possibility of internal hemorrhaging. If your dog has cut his foot or leg badly, on glass or otherwise, bandage the wound as tightly as possible to stop the bleeding. A wad of cotton may serve as a pressure bandage, which will ordinarily stop the flow of blood. Gauze wrapped around the cotton will hold it in place. Usually, applying such pressure to a wound will sufficiently stop the blood flow; however, for severe bleeding, such as when an artery is cut, a tourniquet may be necessary. Apply a tourniquet between the injury and the heart if the bleeding is severe. To tighten the tourniquet, push a pencil through the bandage and twist it. Take your dog to a veterinarian immediately since a tourniquet should not be left in place any longer than fifteen minutes.

Blood coming from an artery is bright red in color and will spurt in unison with the heart beat. From a vein, it is dark red and continuous in flow.

Burns and Scalds

Any dog kept in the home runs the risk of being burned or scalded at one time or another. If your pet sustains a serious burn, call the vet immediately as shock quickly follows such a burn. The dog should be kept warm and quiet, wrapped in a blanket. If he still shows signs of being chilled, use a hot water bottle. Clean the burn gently, removing any foreign matter such as bits of lint, hair, grass or dirt. Act as quickly as possible. Prevent exposure to air by applying olive oil or another similar substance and cover with gauze, cotton and a loose bandage. To prevent the dog from interfering with the dressing, muzzle him and have someone stay with him until veterinary treatment is at hand.

If the burn or scald is a minor one clip hair away from the affected area and apply a paste of bicarbonate of soda and water. Apply it thickly to the burned area and try to keep the dog from licking it off.

Often the only way to adequately determine the best treatment for your dog is through microscopic analysis of a blood smear or tissue scraping so the veterinarian can diagnose the ailment exactly.

Snake Bite

If your dog is bitten by a poisonous snake, open up the wound with any available instrument that is sharp and clean. Squeeze the wound to cause a fair amount of blood to flow. This will wash the poison from the wound as much as possible. The dog should be taken to the veterinarian immediately so antitoxins can be administered. If the bite has been sustained on the leg, it is advisable to apply a tourniquet if at all possible to keep the poison from flowing further. Under no circumstances should snake bite from a poisonous snake, or its treatment, be taken lightly.

Stings

Many dogs enjoy trying to catch wasps and bees. When these insects are prevalent it is difficult to stop your pet from snapping at them. A sting frequently follows a successful catch and it often occurs inside the mouth, which can be very serious. The best remedy is to get him to a veterinarian as soon as possible, but there are some precautionary measures to follow in the meantime. If the dog has been lucky enough to only be caught on the outside of the face, try to extricate the stinger, then swab the point of entry with a solution of bicarbonate of soda. In the case of a wasp sting, use vinegar or some other acidic food stuff. A useful remedy for wasp stings is to rub the part with moistened tobacco, i.e., an unsmoked cigarette end that has been moistened.

IMPORTANCE OF INOCULATIONS

With the proper series of inoculations, your dog will be almost completely protected against disease. However, it occasionally happens that the shot does not take, and sometimes a different form of the virus appears against which your dog may not be protected.

Distemper

Probably the most virulent of all dog diseases is distemper. Young dogs are most susceptible to it, although it may affect dogs of all ages. The dog will lose his appetite, seem depressed, chilled, and run a fever. Often he will have a watery discharge from his eyes and nose. Unless treated promptly, the disease goes into advanced stages with infections of the lungs, intestines, and nervous system, and dogs that recover may be left with some impairment such as paralysis, convulsions, a twitch, or some other defect, usually spastic in nature. The best protection against this is very early inoculation with a series of permanent shots and a booster shot each year thereafter.

Hepatitis

Veterinarians report an increase in the spread of this viral disease in recent years, usually with younger dogs as the victims. The initial symptoms—drowsiness, vomiting, great thirst, loss of appetite, and a high temperature—closely resemble those of distemper. These symptoms are often accompanied by swellings of the head, neck, and abdomen. The disease strikes quickly; death may occur in just a few hours. Protection is afforded by injection with a vaccine recently developed.

Leptospirosis

This disease is carried by bacteria that live in stagnant or slow-moving water. It is carried by rats and dogs; infection is begun by the dog's licking substances contaminated by the urine or feces of infected animals. The symptoms are diarrhea and a yellowish-brownish discoloration of the jaws, tongue, and teeth, caused by an inflammation of the kidneys.

This disease can be cured if caught in time, but it is best to ward it off with a vaccine which your veterinarian can administer along with the distemper shots.

Rabies

This is an acute disease of the dog's central nervous system. It is spread by infectious saliva transmitted by the bite of an infected animal. Rabies is generally manifested in one of two classes of symptoms. The first is "furious rabies," in which the dog shows a period of melancholy or depression, then irritation, and finally paralysis. The first period lasts from a few hours to several days. During this time the dog is cross and will change his position often. He loses his appetite for food and begins to lick, bite and swallow foreign objects. During the irritative phase the dog is spasmodically wild and has impulses to run away. He acts in a fearless manner and runs at and bites everything in sight. If he is caged or confined he will fight at the bars, often breaking teeth or fracturing his jaw. His bark becomes a peculiar howl. In the final, or paralytic, stage, the animal's lower jaw becomes paralyzed and hangs down; he walks with a stagger and saliva drips from his mouth. Within four to eight days after the onset of paralysis, the dog dies.

The second class of symptoms is referred to as "dumb rabies" and is characterized by the dog's walking in a bearlike manner, head down. The lower jaw is paralyzed and the dog is unable to bite. Outwardly, it may seem as though he had a bone caught in his throat.

Even if your pet should be bitten by a rabid dog or other animal, he probably can be saved if you get him to the veterinarian in time for a series of injections. However, after the symptoms have appeared no cure is possible. But remember that an annual rabies inoculation is almost certain protection against rabies. If you suspect that your dog has rabies, notify your local Health Department. A rabid dog is a danger to all who come near him.

Canine Parvovirus

This highly contagious virus disease has recently joined the ranks of potential canine killers and has spread in almost epidemic proportions throughout certain sections of the United States. It has appeared in Canada, Australia and Europe as well. CPV attacks the intestinal tract, white blood cells, and less frequently the heart muscle. It is believed to spread through dog-to-dog contact, the specific source of infection being the fecal waste matter of infected dogs. CPV is particularly hard to overcome because it is capable of existing in the environment for many months under varying conditions unless strong disinfectants are used.

CPV's high degree of contagion is augmented by the fact that it can readily be transmitted from place to place on the hair and feet of infected dogs. Contact with contaminated cages, shoes, and the like can also transmit CPV. However, while it is highly contagious among dogs, the disease cannot be contracted by other animals or people from infected dogs.

The initial signs of infection of this viral disease are normally vomiting and severe diarrhea, which will appear within five to seven days after the individual has been exposed to the virus. At the onset of illness, feces will be light gray or yellow-gray in color. Occasionally, the dog's diarrheal waste will be blood-streaked. Because of the vomiting and severe diarrhea, the dog that has contracted the disease will dehydrate quickly. Depression and loss of appetite can accompany the other symptoms as well as a rise in temperature in younger dogs especially. Temperatures may range from 104 degrees to 106. Older dogs may suffer no temperature increase at all and generally CPV is fatal in only two to three percent of those afflicted.

Death caused by this disease normally occurs within 48 to 72 hours following the appearance of the symptoms. Puppies are hardest hit, with the virus being fatal to 75 percent of puppies that contract it. Death is almost shock-like in their case and can occur within two days of the onset of the illness.

The best preventive measure for CPV is vaccination administered by your veterinarian. Consult him about the duration of immunity of each inoculation and for a schedule of future inoculations. Precautionary measures individual pet owners can take include disinfecting the kennel and other areas where the dog is housed. Since the virus is hardy and capable of existing for many months, a strong disinfectant must be used. One part sodium hypochlorite solution (household bleach), to 30 parts of water will do the job efficiently. Keep the dog from coming into contact with the fecal matter of other dogs when walking or exercising your pet.

HIP DYSPLASIA

This often crippling condition is more prevalent in large breeds than in small, but has occurred in almost every breed. The cause is not absolutely known though it is believed to be hereditary and as yet there is no known cure. The condition exists in varying degrees of severity. In general, hip dysplasia can be described as a poor fit between the two bones of the hip joint—the femur and the acetabulum—and is caused by a malformation of one or the other. Either the head of the femur is flattened causing it to slip out of the socket, or a shallowness of the acetabulum causes the femur to slip out. HD is usually graded according to severity and poorness of fit between the ball and socket, with the lowest grades being the best fit and the higher end of the scale denoting the worst cases.

HD causes stiffness in the hindlegs, considerable pain in the more severe cases and difficulty of movement. It generally manifests itself in puppyhood and can be noticed by the time the young dog is two months old. Severity can usually be determined by the age of six months. If HD is suspected, the dog should be x-rayed, and if afflicted it should not be used for breeding. Cases vary greatly, but severe pain may be more or less continuous in advanced cases. When this is true euthanasia is occasionally recommended, though medication is available to control the pain and allow the dog to move with more ease. Rigorous exercise is not recommended since it only increases the rate at which the bone surfaces wear away.

COUGHS, COLDS, BRONCHITIS, PNEUMONIA

Respiratory diseases may affect the dog because he is forced to live under man-made conditions rather than in his natural environment. Being subjected to cold or a draft after a bath, sleeping near an air conditioner or in the path of a fan or near a radiator can cause respiratory ailments. The symptoms are similar to those in humans. The germs of these diseases, however, are different and do not affect both dogs and humans, so they cannot be infected by each other. Treatment is much the same as for a child with the same type of illness. Keep the dog warm, quiet, and well fed. Your veterinarian has antibiotics and other remedies to help the dog recover.

DIABETES MELLITUS (Sugar Diabetes)

This is a disease wherein the sugar balance of the body is disturbed because of insufficient production of the hormone insulin. The pancreas secretes insulin which regulates carbohydrate/sugar usage. When the insulin-producing cells are damaged, the condition arises. It is marked by an increase in the blood sugar level and an excessive amount of sugar is excreted in the urine.

Symptoms of the condition are great thirst, increased urination and loss of weight while the appetite and food consumption increases. The signs vary in severity. If overlooked, emaciation and collapse rapidly occur. The dog can go into a diabetic coma and die.

Treatment is the same as for human diabetes, utilizing dietary regulation and insulin injections if necessary. The diet should be one of very low fat, with a low percentage of carbohydrate and a higher pecentage of protein. The insulin dose must be adjusted as indicated by urine tests which your veterinarian can teach you to administer at home. The test makes use of chemically treated sticks, pale yellow in color, which turn to various shades of green when dipped in urine. The darker the shade, the more serious the condition.

INTERNAL PARASITES

There are four common internal parasites that may infect your dog. These are roundworms, hookworms, whipworms, and tapeworms. The first three can be diagnosed by laboratory examination; the presence of tapeworms is determined by seeing segments in the stool or attached to the hair around the tail. Do not under any circumstances attempt to worm your dog without the advice of your veterinarian. After first determining what type of worm or worms are present, he will advise you of the best method of treatment.

A dog or puppy in good physical condition is less susceptible to worm infestation than a weak dog. Proper sanitation and a nutritious diet help in preventing worms. One of the best preventative measures is to always have clean, dry bedding for your dog. This will diminish the possibility of reinfection due to flea or tick bites.

Heartworms

Heartworm infestation in dogs is passed by mosquitoes and can be a life threatening problem. Dogs with the disease tire easily, have difficulty breathing, cough and may lose weight despite a hearty appetite. If caught in the early stages, the disease can be effectively treated; however, the administration of daily preventative medicine throughout the spring, summer and fall months is strongly advised. Your veterinarian must first take

Pictured is the heart of a dog showing a heavy infestation of heartworms. Mosquitoes carry the offspring of the adult worms which are implanted into a dog's bloodstream when the dog is bitten. The worm offspring travel to the heart where they do their damage as they develop into adult worms. U.S.D.A.

94

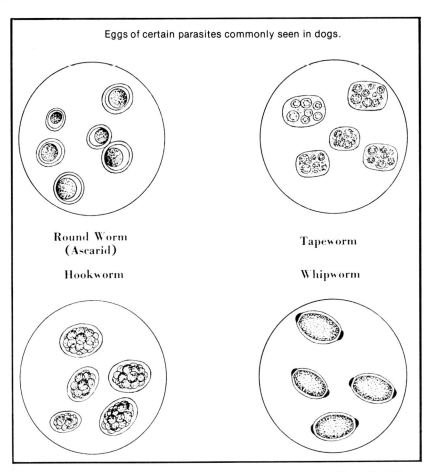

Eggs of certain parasites commonly seen in dogs.

Round Worm
(Ascarid)

Tapeworm

Hookworm

Whipworm

The presence of worms in your dog's system can manifest itself in outward signs such as a general deterioration, loss of weight, dulling of coat, diarrhea and vomiting. *Roundworm* larvae penetrate the intestinal lining, where they enter the bloodstream and are carried to the lungs. This worm affects mostly puppies, in whom it can cause lung damage and intestinal blockage. There are many species of *tapeworm* that can infest your dog. The important factor in breaking the life cycle of the tapeworm is the elimination of the parasitic host on which the worm thrives. Fleas are perhaps the most common host, so ridding your dog of them is a step toward eliminating the possibility of tapeworm infection. If present in massive quantities, *hookworms*, which remove blood from the dog, may cause circulatory collapse and ultimate death. *Whipworms* may cause weight loss, vomiting, diarrhea and secondary anemia in an affected dog.

a blood sample from your dog to test for the presence of the disease, and if the dog is heartworm-free, pills or liquid medicine can be prescribed that will protect against any infestation.

It was formerly believed that heartworms occured only in warmer climates, but it is now known that they may occur anywhere that they can be carried by any of several species of mosquitoes.

Adult worms are found in the right side of the heart, the vena cavae and the pulmonary artery. There the eggs develop and are released as microfilariae. The microfilariae circulate in the blood of the dog until a mosquito ingests them, starting the larval growth cycle. Being carried by the various mosquito species induces the third-stage larval development. The third-stage larvae are re-deposited during a subsequent feeding by the mosquito and proceed to grow.

Microfilariae remain inactive while in the blood of the dog in which they were originally deposited by the female. It is only after they have been ingested by a subsequent mosquito and redeposited in another host that they begin to develop. These larvae lodge in subcutaneous tissue or muscle where they stay about three months; at between three and four months they migrate to the heart. Three to four months later the adult worm begins producing microfilariae.

Adult worms are creamy white in color. The female grows to 11 or 12 inches in length, the male, to six or seven inches. The sexes are distinquished by length since both are about the diameter of the lead in a mechanical pencil. Each mature female worm is capable of producing 30,000 microfilariae each day. A hundred adult females can account for about two billion microfilariae in the body of a dog since microfilariae live up to two years.

Apparently canines of all ages are susceptible to heartworm infestation, but they must have been exposed to mosquitoes in order to have acquired the third-stage infective larvae. Heartworm infection increases markedly as the dog matures. If left undetected, it will erode the heart.

A microscopic search for microfilariae is necessary to prove that adult worms are present. Because of the large number and size of the worms, treatment must be careful and slow to minimize damage to the circulatory system.

SKIN AILMENTS

Any persistent scratching may indicate an irritation. Whenever you groom your dog, look for the reddish spots that may indicate eczema, mange, or fungal infection. Rather than treating your dog yourself, take him to the veterinarian, as some of the conditions may be difficult to eradicate and can cause permanent damage to his coat.

Two of the most common external parasites are the tick (left) and the flea (right). Along with the general discomfort and irritation that they bring to your dog, these parasites can infest him with worms and disease. The flea is a carrier of tapeworm, and may act as an intermediate host for heartworm. The tick can cause dermatitis and anemia in your dog, and may also be a carrier of Rocky Mountain spotted fever and canine babesiasis, a blood infection.

External Parasites

The dog that is groomed regularly and provided with clean sleeping quarters should not be troubled by fleas, ticks, or lice. If the dog should become infested with any of these parasites, he should be treated with medicated dip bath or the new oral medications that are presently available.

Mange

There are two types of mange, sarcoptic and follicular, both of which are caused by a parasite. The former is by far the more common, and results in an intense irritation, causing violent scratching. Close examination will reveal small red spots which become filled with pus. This is a highly contagious condition, and any dog showing signs of the disease should be isolated. Consult your veterinarian for the proper treatment procedures. Follicular mange is very much harder to cure, but fortunately, it is much rarer and less contagious. This disease will manifest itself as bare patches appearing on the skin, which becomes thickened and leathery. A complete cure from this condition is only rarely effected.

Eczema

This disease occurs most often in the summer months and affects the dog down the back, especially just above the root of the tail. It should not be confused with mange, as it is not caused by a parasite. One of the principle causes of eczema is improper nutrition, which makes the dog susceptible to disease. Hot, humid weather predisposes the growth of bacteria, which can invade a susceptible dog and thereby cause skin irritations and lesions. It is imperative that the dog gets relief from the itching that is symptomatic of the disease as this self-mutilation by scratching will only help to spread the inflammation. Antibiotics may be necessary if a bacterial infection is, indeed, present. The dog must be thoroughly ridded of fleas to avoid any recurrance of the scratching that can spread the disease.

Moist eczema, commonly referred to as "hot spots," is a rapidly appearing skin disease that produces a moist infection. Spots appear very suddenly and may spread rapidly in a few hours, infecting several parts of the body. These lesions are generally bacterially infected and are extremely itchy, which will cause the dog to scratch frantically and further damage the afflicted areas. Vomiting, fever and an enlargement of the lymph nodes may occur. The infected areas must be clipped to the skin and thoroughly cleaned. Your veterinarian will prescribe an anti-inflammatory drug and antibiotics, as well as a soothing emollient to relieve itching.

EYES, EARS, TEETH AND NAILS

If your dog is to remain in good health, you must be aware of the need for periodic "examinations" in which you routinely inspect him for unusual signs of irritation or infection. In most cases, the tell-tale warning signals are any unusual swelling, discharge or redness that may appear, especially after an injury.

The eyes, because of their sensitivity, are prone to injury and infection. Dogs that spend a great deal of time outdoors in heavily wooded areas may return from an exercise excursion with watery eyes, the result of brambles and high weeds scratching them. The eyes may also be irritated by dirt and other foreign matter.

Should your dog's eyes appear red and watery, a mild solution can be mixed at home for a soothing washing. Your veterinarian will be able to tell you what percentage of boric acid, salt, or other medicinal compound to mix with water.

You must monitor your dog's eyes after such a solution is administered; if the irritation persists, or if there is a significant discharge, immediate veterinary attention is warranted.

Your dog's ears, like his eyes, are extremely sensitive and can also be prone to infection, should wax and/or dirt be allowed to build up. Ear irritants may be present in the form of mites, soap or water, or foreign par-

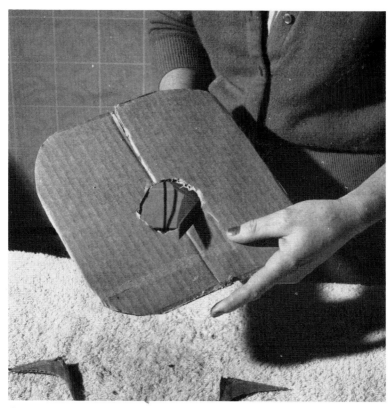

The Elizabethan collar is designed to keep your dog from scratching the area about his head and ears when a wound or sutures there advise against scratching. While they can be purchased ready-made, they can also be easily made at home from a piece of cardboard box. Be sure the hole is large enough so that it does not constrict the dog's breathing or swallowing.

ticles which the dog has come into contact with while romping through a wooded area. If your dog's ears are bothering him, you will know it—he will scratch and paw them, shake his head, and the ears will show a foul-smelling dark secretion. This pasty secretion usually signals the onset of *otorrhea*, or ear canker, and at this stage proper veterinary care is essential if the dog's hearing is not to be permanently impaired. In the advanced stages of ear canker, tissue builds up within the ear, and the ear canal becomes blocked off, thus eliminating the hearing abilities of that ear.

If this is to be prevented, you should wash your dog's ears as they require it, with a very dilute solution of hydrogen peroxide and water, or an antibacterial ointment, as your vet suggests. In any case, the ears, because of their delicacy, are to be washed gently, with a soft cloth or cotton.

The good health of your pet's teeth can be maintained by his regular use of a chew product such as Nylabone® or Nylaball®, which serves to clean the teeth of tartar accumulation and massage and stimulate the gums. With puppies, a chew product helps to relieve the discomfort of the teething stage, and of course prevents the pup's chewing of your furniture and slippers!

A periodic inspection of your dog's mouth will alert you to any problem he might have that would require a trip to the veterinarian's office. Any signs of tooth or gum sensitivity, redness or swelling, signal the need for professional treatment. Also, it is best to have your pet's teeth scraped once or twice a year, at the time that he goes to the vet's for his general physical check-up. This simple procedure removes any excess tartar that

Badly decayed teeth can cause abscesses of mouth tissues and gums, and even bone deterioration in extreme cases. Pain caused by such a condition can discourage your dog from eating even though he is hungry, resulting in possible malnutrition or even starvation. Your vet should be consulted if any listlessness or change in eating habits is noticed.

Dog nail clippers are designed to trim nails quickly and easily with a minimum of scuffling between you and your dog. While other general purpose instruments can be used, there is a greater chance with these of cutting too far down on the nail and hitting the vein, resulting in a painful experience for your dog.

has accumulated on his teeth that could cause degeneration of tooth enamel, if left to build up.

If you live in a city and walk your dog regularly on pavement, chances are that his nails are kept trimmed from the "wear and tear" they receive from the sidewalks. However, if your dog gets all of his exercise in your yard, or if his nails simply grow rather quickly, it will occasionally be necessary for you to clip his nails. It is best for you to have your veterinarian show you the proper way to perform the nail clipping at first. Special care must always be taken to avoid cutting too far and reaching the "quick." If you cut into the quick of the nail, it will bleed, so it is easy to see why an expert must show you the proper procedure. A nail clipper designed especially for dogs can be purchased at any pet shop.

CARE OF THE AGED DOG

With the increased knowledge and care available, there is no reason why your dog should not live to a good old age. As the years go by he may need a little additional care. Remember that an excessively fat dog is not healthy, particularly as he grows older, so limit the older dog's food accordingly. He needs exercise as much as ever, although his heart cannot bear the strain of sudden and violent exertion. Failing eyesight or hearing means lessened awareness of dangers, so you must protect him more than ever.

Should you decide at this time to get a puppy, to avoid being without a dog when your old friend is no longer with you, be very careful how you introduce the puppy. He naturally will be playful and will expect the older dog to respond to his advances. Sometimes the old dog will get a new lease on life from a new puppy, but he may be consumed with jealousy. Do not give the newcomer the attention that formerly was exclusively the older dog's. Feed them apart, and show your old friend that you still love him the most; the puppy, not being accustomed to individual attention, will not mind sharing your love.

TATTOOING

Tattooing is an increasingly popular method of identifying your dog that has met with growing success in assuring the safe return of lost or stolen dogs. Several registries exist that will record a dog's tattoo number along with his owner's name, address and telephone number. Two types of tattoo numbers can be assigned. In the case of mixed breed dogs, the owner's social security number is generally used; in the case of pedigreed dogs, the dog's AKC registration number is used. These two numbers are the most common means of identification. The groin or inside of the ear is the usual spot for the tattoo mark, though cases have been cited in which a dog's ear was cut off to eliminate the possibility of catching the dognappers.

For a minor fee, your veterinarian can do the simple, painless job that may insure the return of a beloved pet or show dog. Such return would be reward enough for the few minutes it takes to have this simple procedure done. Since a puppy grows very rapidly, it is best not to have him tattooed until he is at least four months old to avoid any possible smearing of the tattoo ink. There is almost no danger of infection if the job is done properly and exhibitors run no risk of having the show dog's career impaired by the tattoo mark since the AKC has ruled that no judge may disqualify or penalize a dog because of a tattoo.

Your local kennel club will be able to supply the name of a registry in your area.

9. DOG SHOW COMPETITION

There is no greater pleasure for the owner than showing a beautiful dog perfectly groomed and trained for the show ring. Whether he wins or not, it is gratifying to show a dog in superb condition, one that is a credit to your training and care. A great deal of preparation, both for you and your dog, is needed before the day that you do any serious winning. Showing is not as easy as it looks, even if you have a magnificent dog. He must be presented to the judge so that all of his good points are shown to advantage. This requires practice in gaiting, daily grooming from puppyhood, and the proper diet to make him sound in body.

When you buy your puppy you probably will think he is the best in the country and possibly in the world, but before you enter the highly competitive world of dog shows, get an unbiased expert opinion. Visit a few dog shows as a spectator and make mental notes of what is required of the handlers and dogs. Watch how the experienced handlers manage their dogs to bring out their best points.

HOW TO SELECT A SHOW DOG

If you are planning to show your dog, it is best not to buy a puppy any younger than four or six months of age. Since it is difficult at best to predict what a puppy will look like at maturity, you cannot rely wholly on its appearance while it is only six or eight weeks old. By doing a certain amount of homework before purchasing your show dog, you can be assured to an extent that you will end up with a show quality dog that will hold its own in the show rings. Before going out to buy, read some good books on your breed. Consult a reputable book of standards for the breed to get an idea of what the dog should look like as an adult. Remember that no individual dog ever completely achieves the standard, but knowing the important conformational points of the breed will help to illustrate what you are aiming for in your show dog. Attending dog shows and talking with veterans who have been in the dog game for a while will give you valuable information to use when choosing your own show prospect.

One of the best assurances you can get in a field where there are no real guarantees is to search out well-known breeders who are known to have successfully bred show winners through several generations. Ask to look at the pedigree of any puppy you are considering buying, noting whether there are numerous top-quality dogs in the ancestry. Have the sire and

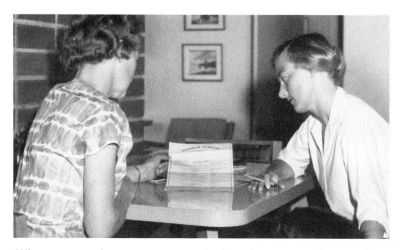

When you purchase your puppy, the breeder can supply you with a pedigree for him. A puppy of champion bloodlines is often of superior quality.

dam of the litter you are interested in been bred before, and if so, what was the overall quality of their previous offspring? If they have produced consistently good dogs through several of the same pairings, your chances of getting a good specimen are fairly high. If the stud or bitch, or both, are unproven in previous litters, the probability of attaining top quality in the puppies is less likely.

In general, the rule of thumb to follow is to go by the expertise of the breeder. A reputable breeder will sell you the best dog possible if you make it clear to him that the dog will definitely be used for a show career. The show contender you purchase not only represents you as its owner, but also reflects the quality of the kennel of the breeder. The reputation of both exhibitor and breeder is made by the quality of the dogs they present, so careful selection of a show dog is essential to all involved.

TYPES OF DOG SHOWS

There are various types of dog shows. The American Kennel Club sanctioned matches are shows at which purebred dogs may compete, but not for championship points. These are excellent for you to enter to accustom you and your dog to showing. If your dog places in a few match shows, then you might seriously consider entering the big-time shows. An American Kennel Club all-breed show is one at which purebred dogs compete for championship points. An American Kennel Club specialty show is for one breed only. It may be held in conjunction with an all-breed show (by designating the classes at that show as its specialty show) or it may be held entirely apart. Obedience trials are different in that in them the dog is judged according to his obedience and ability to perform, not by his conformation to the breed standard.

There are two types of championship conformation shows: *benched* and *unbenched*. At a benched show your dog must be on his appointed bench during the advertised hours of the show's duration. He may be removed from the bench only to be taken to the exercise pen or to be groomed (an hour before the showing) in an area designated for handlers to set up their crates and grooming tables. At an unbenched show your car may serve as a bench for your dog.

To become a champion your dog must win fifteen points in competition with other dogs; a portion of the fifteen points must be awarded as major point wins (three to five points) under different judges.

This scene from a large indoor show captures the exciting moment when the group winners go before the judge for the Best In Show competition.

HOW TO ENTER

If your dog is purebred and registered with the AKC—or eligible for registration—you may enter him in the appropriate show class for which his age, sex, and previous show record qualify him. You will find coming shows listed in the different dog magazines or at your petshop. Write to the secretary of the show, asking for the premium list. When you receive the entry form, fill it in carefully and send it back with the required entry fee. Then, before the show, you should receive your exhibitor's pass, which will admit you and your dog to the show. Here are the five official show classes:

PUPPY CLASS: Open to dogs at least six months and not more than twelve months of age. Limited to dogs whelped in the United States and Canada.

NOVICE CLASS: Open to dogs six months of age or older that have never won a first prize in any class other than puppy class, and less than three first prizes in the novice class itself. Limited to dogs whelped in the United States or Canada.

BRED BY EXHIBITOR CLASS: Open to all dogs, except cham-

To transport your dog long distances, crates should be used that have been made especially for that purpose. They are designed to give your dog optimum ventilation and comfort, while still assuring his maximum safety and protection.

Your pet store carries a large number of pet feeding and watering bowls, in sizes suitable for any size dog. While at a show, be sure to supply your dog with a light meal and some fresh water to keep him comfortable.

pions, six months of age or over which are exhibited by the same person, or his immediate family, or kennel that was the recognized breeder on the records of the American Kennel Club.

AMERICAN-BRED CLASS: Open to dogs that are not champions, six months of age or over, whelped in the United states after a mating which took place in the United States.

OPEN CLASS: Open to dogs six months of age or over, with no exceptions.

In addition there are local classes, the Specials Only class, and brace and team entries.

For full information on dog shows, read the book *How to Show Your Own Dog,* by Virginia Tuck Nichols. (T.F.H.)

JUNIOR SHOWMANSHIP

If you have considered that you and your dog are going to go the show route, you might consider having your youngster show the dog in the ring. If your child has an especially good relationship with his pet, or if he has trained the dog himself, as many children do, then Junior Showmanship might be a good learning experience.

Junior Showmanship is competition among children of different age groups, handling dogs owned by their immediate families. The age divisions are: Novice A, for 10 to 12 year olds; Novice B, for those boys and girls from 13 to 16 (entrants in these two classes must have one or no prior Junior Showmanship wins); Open A for those 10 to 12 years of age; Open B for those 13 to 16 (these entrants must have earned two or more Junior Showmanship awards).

Children involved in JS have the wonderful opportunity to feel a sense of achievement and victory, should they walk away with the ribbons after a show. Even still, winning is not the most important factor here: the pride and responsibility the youngster feels at having reached the ring is surely worth the effort and discipline required to enter showmanship competition.

For more information on JS, and to obtain a rules and regulations booklet, you can contact the American Kennel Club in New York.

ADVANCED PREPARATION

Before you go to a show your dog should be trained to gait at a trot beside you, with head up and in a straight line. In the ring you will have to gait your dog around the edge with other dogs and then individually up and down the center runner. In addition the dog must stand for ex-

If yours is intended to be a show dog, you will want to be prepared with all the tools and equipment necessary for the meticulous grooming of a show dog. Several different types of combs, brushes, clippers and coat grooming products can be obtained from the local pet store.

Be sure to take along a comfortable carrier for your dog if he is to be confined, or benched, during the show's duration.

amination by the judge, who will look at him closely and feel his head and body structure. He should be taught to stand squarely, hind feet slightly back, head up on the alert. Showing requires practice training sessions in advance. Get a friend to act as judge and set the dog up and "show" him a few minutes every day.

Sometime before the show, give your dog a bath so he will look his best. Get together all the things you will need to take to the show. You will want to take a water dish and a bottle of water for your dog (so he won't be affected by a change in drinking water). Take your show lead, bench chain (if it is a benched show), combs and brush, and the identification ticket sent by the show superintendent, noting the time you must be there and the place where the show will be held, as well as the time of judging.

THE DAY OF THE SHOW

Don't feed your dog the morning of the show, or give him at most a light meal. He will be more comfortable in the car on the way, and will show more enthusiastically. When you arrive at the show grounds, find out where he is to be benched and settle him there. Your bench or stall

Conformation to the ideal standard for the breed will be recognized in show dogs by the awarding of ribbons and trophies. Dog show entrants can win on several different levels, with the most significant and exciting award being Best In Show honors.

number is on your identification ticket, and the breed name will be on placards fastened to the ends of the row of benches. Once you have your dog securely fastened to his stall by a bench chain (use a bench crate instead of a chain if you prefer), locate the ring where your dog will be judged (the number and time of showing will be on the program of judging which came with your ticket). After this you may want to take your dog to the exercise ring to relieve himself, and give him a small drink of water. Your dog will have been groomed before the show, but give him a final brushing just before going into the show ring. When your breed judging is called, it is your responsibility to be at the ringside ready to go in. The steward will give you an armband which has on it the number of your dog.

Then, as you step into the ring, try to keep your knees from knocking! Concentrate on your dog and before you realize it you'll be out again, perhaps back with the winners of each class for more judging and finally, with luck, it will be over and you'll have a ribbon and trophy—and, of course, the most wonderful dog in the world!

10. BUILDING A KENNEL AND EXERCISE RUNS

DRAWING UP PLANS

Whether you have one dog or many, the time may come when you decide that an outdoor kennel and runs will best satisfy your dog's exercise and housing needs. Properly built and maintained, a kennel offers your dog the comfort of dry living quarters, adequate ventilation and sunlight, and the availability of regular exercise.

Before you begin to draw up plans for kennel construction, check with your town's municipal offices to see if a building permit is required and which, if any, regulations of the building code you must adhere to. The permit, if required, must be obtained before any construction is begun. Building a kennel is not a small undertaking, so pre-planning on all fronts will prevent unexpected snags from cropping up, causing time delays and inconveniences.

One of the first decisions to make concerns the choice between building the kennel yourself as a sort of family project, or hiring a general contractor to do the work. If you decide on the latter, details of financing, building plans and blueprints to suit your needs should be worked out before contractual agreements are signed. For the plans on actual construction, including a concrete foundation, framework and overall structure, you should consult an architect who will, for a fee, draw up a set of blueprints for you or a contractor to follow. Have the architect see your land, and detail clearly to him each specific feature you want designed into the building. In this way you will enable him to set down a precise set of blueprints, meeting your specifications.

LAND AND SPACE REQUIREMENTS

To build an average size kennel, you must have a significant parcel of land to set aside for this purpose. The location of the building site should provide adequate sunlight and shade for warmth and coolness throughout the seasons. The soil should be of a high gravel content as a gravel soil provides good drainage. By comparison, a sandy soil, though its surface dries quickly, retains dampness and residual dirt just beneath the surface. It is also a favorite breeding place of fleas and similar pests.

Drainage is a prime consideration, not only to let natural ground water run off, but also to let the water drain off from the frequent hosings a kennel must be given to ensure cleanliness and prevent growth of disease-producing germs. A kennel should be trenched for drainage much the way a soldier trenches around his tent. One continuous drainage ditch approximately eight inches wide should be dug around all sides of the kennel, no further than a foot away from the kennel walls. It should be dug to a depth of four inches to start with, sloping an additional inch for every three yards of land. With ditches extending from at least two front corners of the building down to this surrounding ditch, water will run away from the building to the lowest point of land, preventing moisture build-up or preventing the water to lay near the kennel building itself. The drainage system can be sophisticated further, the ditch tiled, for instance, and eventually connecting with or running to a storm drain. Whatever else is devised, drainage should definitely figure into your building plans.

BUILDING MATERIALS

The building materials you use are of great importance. Not only must they be of good quality but they must be of a type that will protect the dog from the elements. For example, sheet metal, a conductor of both heat and cold, should never be used for the outside walls or ceilings. It becomes extremely hot in the sun and will retain heat in the kennel, making a potentially dangerous and certainly uncomfortable situation for the dogs. Outside walls should ideally be constructed from lumber, bricks or cinder blocks. The walls must be insulated with a substance that will serve equally well in all seasons, protecting your dogs from the heat and the cold.

Interior walls can be constructed of wood, plywood or plaster board. Plywood has the advantage of being extremely durable; however, plywood is quite expensive and can give way to splintering should the dogs scratch at it. Plaster board, also commonly known as sheet rock, is inexpensive and relatively durable. Plaster board does not, however, stand up well to moisture, but more than compensates for this drawback by being very resistant to insect and rodent infestation.

The above plans detail the probable steps involved in the construction of a rather large kennel, suited for up to a dozen dogs. At first, most dog owners have only one or two dogs that they want to provide for. If this is the case, a large dog house, modified somewhat, will aptly serve until such time that a larger kennel is needed.

THE SINGLE DOG HOUSE

While a dog will be contented with less living space than his master is accustomed to, his own house should be large enough to allow for free space around and above him when he stands up in the enclosure. The size of the dog house depends, of course, on the size of the dog.

Using materials purchased from any lumber store, you can build a dog house yourself. When constructing the house, take care to finish it off well, leaving no nails or wood splinters protruding from the wood which could injure the dog.

If you wish to move your pet into a new, ready-to-go home, finished dog houses can be purchased in varying styles and price ranges. Your pet shop may have some houses in stock; if not, the owner can probably suggest an outlet where one would be available. The yellow pages of your phone directory may also be useful in locating an establishment that carries dog houses, either constructed or in kits. Some of the latest styles available are quite pleasing to the eye, such as the house constructed out of unstripped logs, designed to give your dog his own little log cabin! If you check various outlets you will find that dog houses range in design from the simple to the elaborate.

CARE OF THE DOG HOUSE

To prevent dampness and to retain heat in the dog house, it should not be placed directly on the ground, but elevated at least several inches. A 2″ x 4″ beam placed under two opposing sides of the house, with the 4″ side lying flat on the ground, should allow for proper ventilation beneath the structure. However, in winter months you will want to close off this space to prevent drafts. In this case, boards can easily and quickly be nailed between the 2″ x 4″'s already in place to cover the exposed openings. Keeping the dog house a proper distance from the ground also serves to prevent the possibility of water damage, which will cause the wood to warp and eventually decay. Infestation of the wood by insects can be prevented by keeping the primary wood of the house from contact with the dirt below.

Whether kept in the yard or in the garage, the single dog house has the advantage of being able to be moved from spot to spot. Moving the dog house will be necessary occasionally for such reasons as cleaning, moving into or out of direct sunlight or shade, etc. This is an advantage when you consider that in the cold winter months your dog may very much appreciate having his house placed in direct sunlight! In cold weather the dog house can be positioned with the entranceway facing east or south, to receive full sunlight.

If a shifting of position is all that is needed, a strong friend or two should be able to help relocate the house. However, if the move is for a considerable distance and your dog house is quite heavy, a moving dolly may be necessary.

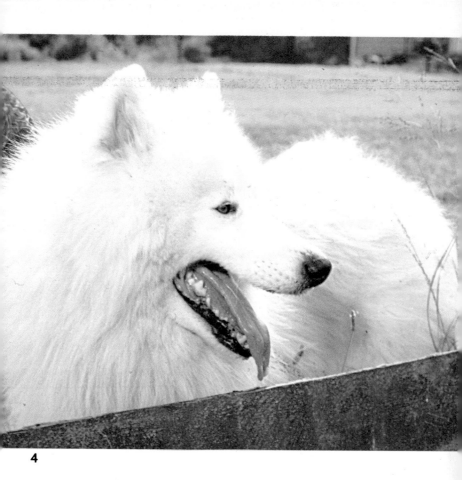

4

(1) Shows one type of kenneling arrangement where many dogs are involved. All outside runs are attached to a single building with inside partitions separating each dog's quarters. The swinging door shown is a good one to keep cold winds out of the building, especially good if inside quarters are not heated. (2) Inside, a tile floor or one of similar material that is maintenance free is a good place to keep your youngster. (3) When puppies are first weaned, one plate may serve for several pups; however, when they are older, each should have his own dish to ensure his fair share. (4) A Sammy peers over the fence of his outdoor enclosure. Where only one Samoyed is owned, a full-fledged kennel and run are not really necessary, but a fenced-in area is ideal for outdoor exercise.

115

The best type of roof for a dog house is a flat or sloping one which can be easily removed or opened at a hinge for cleaning, or to provide the dog with air and sunlight in the warmer months. A sloping roof does not allow excessive rain or snow to accumulate on the top and pose the possible hazard of having the roof collapse under the weight. When constructing the roof, or when purchasing the dog house, remember that it must be properly insulated from the elements. The most efficient form of all-weather protection is tarred roofing paper, covered by good shingles.

The entrance to the dog house is an important item for consideration. It must allow for easy passage at will, and yet protect the dog from bitter drafts. A heavy piece of carpeting or burlap can be nailed above the doorway with a strip of wood to hold it in place. Such a door covering can be used for most of the year, but if you choose to keep your dog outside for any length of time when the weather turns cold, a heavier, more permanent door may become necessary. This too, should allow free movement in and out. A door that swings from hinges placed at the top of the opening is best for this purpose.

Basic obedience training or "backyard" training makes any dog a more acceptable companion. This picture demonstrates the proper direction a chain-link choke collar should be worn if it is to release readily when the dog is not straining against it during training sessions.

Where a grassy area is not available, a fenced-in cement or dirt area will serve the Samoyed's exercise needs. It is important with a smaller area of cement or dirt to clean up after your dog daily.

For warmth and absorption of moisture in inclement weather, place several layers of shredded newspapers or cedar shavings on the floor. In the colder months, several inches of straw placed under a heavy blanket should be sufficient to keep your dog warm. Shreddings should be changed at least once a week, and more often in wet weather.

EXERCISE RUNS

If you want to let your dog out to exercise himself, yet do not care to fence in your entire property, wire runs are in order. The width of the runway should be at least a little more than the length of the dog; the length can be as long as the ground permits. The rule to follow is that any exercise run should be long enough to allow the dog to break into a short gallop. The runway grounds can be made of gravel, cement, or grass and natural ground. Cement and gravel runs provide quick drainage, whereas grass and dirt retain excrement and decayed food and become muddy with rain. If you choose to have natural runs, they must be dug and respaded twice a year. Many dog owners prefer to have cement foundations extend a few feet from the building, the rest of the run being grass. These short foundations can also be used as outdoor feeding places.

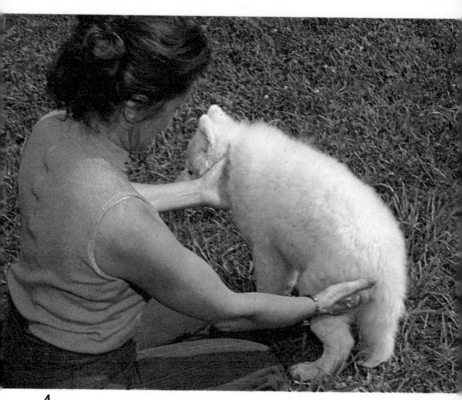

4 About three months is a good age to introduce your dog to the basics of obedience training. It is important to remember, however, not to expect too much from him while he is young and not to extend the training sessions beyond ten minutes at the most. The well-bred Samoyed responds to a gentle touch and balks at heavy-handed methods. (1) The youngster is made to sit in heel position as a prelude to learning the "Heel" command. (2) He is introduced to walking at "Heel." A gentle tug back into position if he wanders too wide or in front of you is effective. (3) A long lead is generally used to teach a dog the "Come" command. If you enjoy a very good rapport with your dog, you may be able to entice him to come using encouraging words and gestures, as the woman above, finally teaching him to associate the word with the action. (4) Here, the owner teaches the young Sam to "Sit," by putting just enough pressure against the knee joint so that he cannot support his weight in the rear quarter and goes naturally into a sitting position. This action accompanied by the word "Sit" soon teaches the dog to associate the word with the act. Some owners prefer this method of teaching this command over the more generally used one of pushing down at the base of the dog's spine, because it is less forceful.

119

An obviously satisfied Samoyed owner, Carol Nissim is pictured with her pup of 5½ months, Northwinds Blue Star.

11. MENTAL AND PHYSICAL GOOD HEALTH

Let's take a look at this beautiful ball of white fluff. Assuming you have purchased a pup from a reputable breeder, we can further assume that it is healthy, well bred and properly socialized. Now all you have to do is sit back and admiringly watch the pup grow, right? WRONG! The next few weeks will determine whether you have the best companion you've ever had or the biggest pain in the neck.

While you will be busy helping him to learn house manners and what is and isn't O.K. behavior, it's important to remember that canines are creatures of habit. That means that every new behavior should be scrutinized and thought of in terms of, "How cute will I think that is when this youngster is a full grown adult?" Puppies chewing on furniture or shoes may be "adorable" to some but that pup is learning that it's O.K. to chew on furniture and shoes! Chew toys of his own are in order and present a good attention diversion which will satisfy his need to chew and save Aunt Abigail's heirloom china closet.

MENTAL MUSCLE

The canine brain has been found to be fully developed by the time a pup is seven weeks of age. That's pretty staggering when you stop to think about it. Between the age of seven weeks and twelve weeks, most of the lifetime patterns of behavior—or habits—are being formed.

You can actually help your pup develop his native intelligence during this time. By presenting him with simple challenges, investigators have found that a pup will grow up with more ability to learn and an easier adaptability to new situations than littermates who have no such experience. The thing to keep in mind when you set up these situations for your pup is that they must be simple enough for him to succeed!

TEST SITUATIONS

With very young pups the introduction of a new squeak toy can be used as a learning tool. Give the toy a good squeak and put it down near the pup. Observe his actions. Does he bounce right to it, or does he shy away, preferring not to investigate? Place a mirror at floor level and make the same observations.

The kind of stress-recovery is limited only by your own imagination. Keep any such experiences limited to no more than five minutes in any

1   2

3 ►

(1) The normally trusting nature of the Samoyed will emerge greatly as he matures from the puppy that has been treated kindly and exposed to much handling when very young. (2) Show handling will be accepted with no resistance if the Samoyed has been exposed to it from a very young age. (3) Rough and tumble with half-grown Sams, while lots of fun can also become overwhelming when the dogs reach this size.

day. By the way, once a week training will also net good results. The object is *success* and be sure to keep the session short.

Trainers at the Morris Foundation for the blind find the two most significant intelligence indicators are the "fetch" and "wheeled cart" tests.

Fetch is just what you think it is. You toss a small ball a few feet away and say, "Puppy, fetch". The thing you're looking for is how quickly the puppy learns he is to go get the ball and bring it back to you.

The wheeled cart takes some help. Puppy should be walking on leash with you while someone else has the cart, preferably out of sight. As you walk along, the second person darts out with the cart to block your path. Does the puppy recover from his startled reaction and does he know enough to continue around the cart? If he is frightened be sure to comfort him and encourage him to complete the task, if possible. Never force a pup who reacts in the extreme.

Other simple challenges, would consist of a broomstick across his path where he has to figure out how to go over it (keep in mind that it must be placed low enough so that he can go over it easily), an empty coffee can with pebbles inside set down on its side, the sudden 'roar' of the vacuum cleaner. All of these are excellent mind builders. Desirable qualities are displayed if the pup comes back after his initial fright at the shopping cart to cautiously investigate. Is he willing to risk going near the coffee can when it is "quiet"? Is he curious? Curiosity is a good quality.

Another interesting challenge is to place two empty fruit crates on their sides at a 45 degree angle to each other. Place the pup inside this very simple maze. Go to the closed end and see how long it takes puppy to figure out how to walk out the open end. Remember, don't leave him frustrated if he doesn't get the hang of it. Walk around to the open side and coax him out with kind words—help him succeed—and be sure to praise him for his efforts.

The most important aspect of any of these challenges is to take it easy, make it fun and keep it short. No longer than five minutes. Both of you will come away, each with a better understanding of the other, and a little smarter than when you began.

GETTING PHYSICAL

There are a great many things that you can see on the outside of your dog that tell you something about what's going on on the inside. For instance, is his coat dull and dry or shiny bright? Are his eyes sparkling or do they run? Is he listless or is he his bubbling self? Is he licking or biting his legs or other parts? Does he shake his head as if something is in his ear? Is his breath O.K.? Does he "scoot" across the floor on his tail? Is his urine normal or is it acrid? How about his stool? Is it well formed or mushy? When he gets up does he *get up* or does he pull himself up using his forequarters alone? Does he limp or trot along?

These things tell you whether your dog is healthy or not. If any one of these signs persist you should consult with your veterinarian immediately.

There are virtually any number of things you'll become aware of as you and your pup grow together but there are things you just can't see. A check-up, stool analysis and hip X-ray are the only sure way to continued good health.

If your dog isn't well the vet can medicate him, if he has worms, they can be eliminated. If his hips are dysplastic or his eyes going blind from PRA (progressive retinal atrophy) you can help him live within a framework that will accommodate his disability. A talk with your veterinarian and some old fashioned common sense will take you and your pup a long way together.

One test of a puppy's intelligence is to create a simple maze using orange crates, then watch how long it takes him to figure his route to freedom. (1) The pup tries to barge out through the side but does not fit—a common mistake. (2) Success! The pup figures the right way out.